Memories; or, the chronicles of Birkenhead, etc. [With illustrations.]

Hilda Gamlin

MEMORIES OF BIRKENHEAD

HILDA GAMLIN

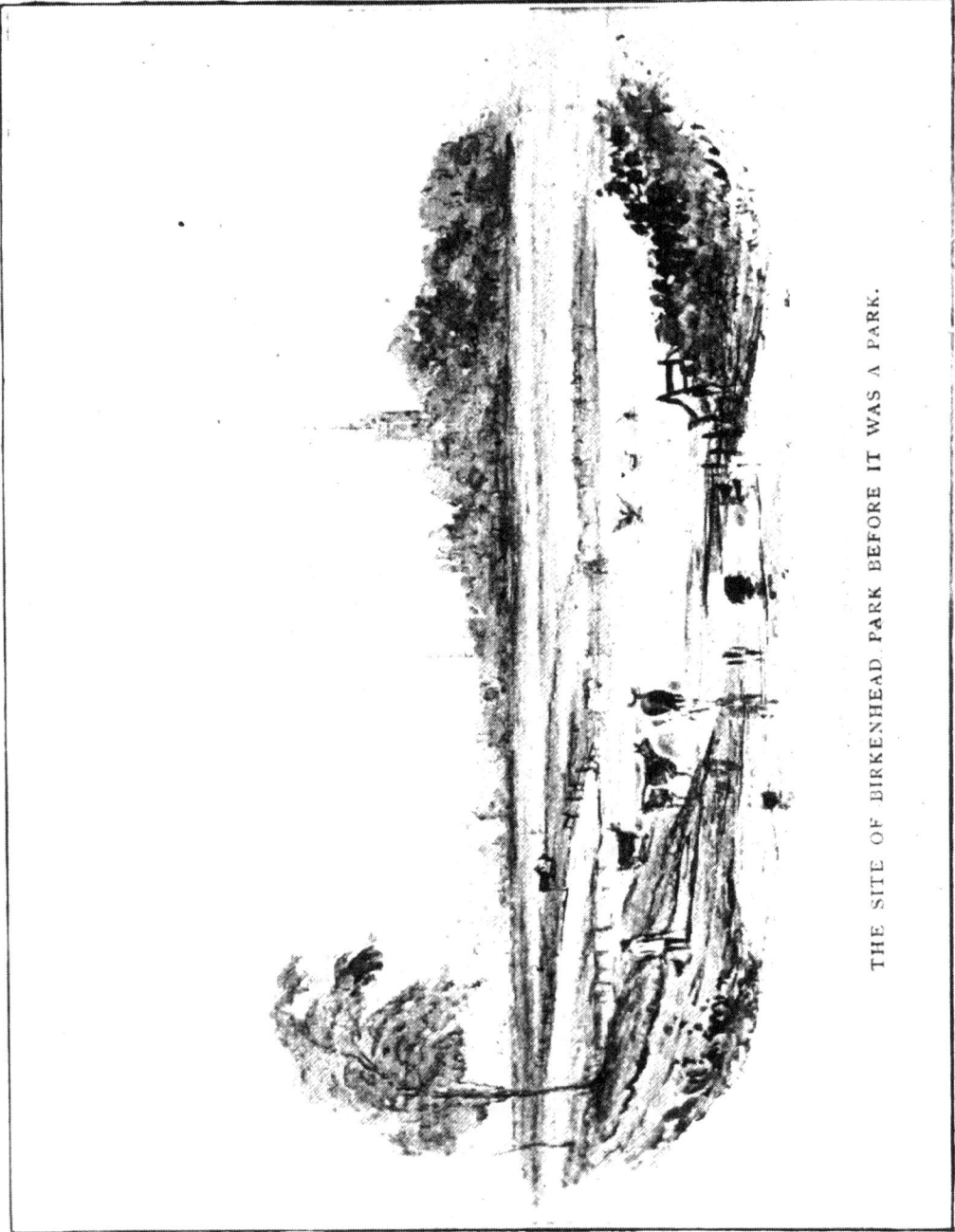

THE SITE OF BIRKENHEAD PARK BEFORE IT WAS A PARK.

MEMORIES

OR

THE CHRONICLES OF BIRKENHEAD

THE SCENES AND PEOPLE OF ITS EARLY DAYS

BY

HILDA GAMLIN

AUTHORESS OF "MEMOIRS OF EMMA LADY HAMILTON."

"Tell me the Tales I delighted to hear, long, long ago,"
OLD SONG

LIVERPOOL

EDWARD HOWELL, 28 CHURCH STREET

1892.

PREFACE

NOTHING has a happier tendency to bring together all classes of a community than the production of a history of its village, town or city, as the case may be. The eagerness with which each one individually welcomes its advent forcibly demonstrates that all grades of society, treading their course in every conceivable pathway of life, have, after all, one common interest—the prosperity of their locality. In considering our own surroundings for the moment, we find that scientific enterprise has so rapidly obliterated the rural scenes of Birkenhead as to cause it to be typified as a town of "mushroom" growth. Regarding its rise, the appellation conveys no sneer, for a mushroom is a very good thing, but the edible fungus is short-lived and soon perishes, and herein lies the simile that alone could contain reproach. That the town could start up from the obscurity of generations and make a name for itself, but, being unable to retain its position, should relapse into worse than its original nothingness, marked as a failure, while every other modern town shows progress and prosperity, there would lie the covert significance against which we must contend.

Said the mushroom that had sprung up in the night to the great oak tree that had flourished for centuries, "Are you thinking where I was yesterday?" "No" replied the monarch of the forest, "I am wondering where you will be to-morrow."

Fabulous wealth is attributed to many residents of

the district, yet the community at large seems to
benefit little by its circulation. No important effort is
made by these successful business men to advance the
prosperity of the town of their adoption, which contains every scope for enlarging and retaining its name
in capital letters on the map of England. Lethargy
pervades the higher social powers to an extent unparalleled in no other equally populous district. Would
it not conduce to their own aggrandisement if they
could assert, with conscious pride, that Birkenhead is
their dwelling-place ? The dormant condition of trade
is considered by outsiders to be a grave reflection upon
the upper ranks, who should hold it a conscientious
duty to advance local interest in preference to that of
an alien.

If an infusion of sympathy and kind feeling could
be induced to circulate, what a different tale may not
the next historian tell! No half measures achieve
great ends. Goodwill and energy can revive the fallen
fortunes of Birkenhead, and recall the brightness and
brotherhood that existed in the days of long ago.

In concluding this prefatory matter, I desire to
return thanks to the Birkenhead Library Committee,
who have courteously allowed the reproduction of a
drawing in their possession, "The site of Birkenhead
Park before it was a Park." They retain the right
of reproduction of this drawing beyond this book. To
the Librarians also I beg to express my obligation for
literary assistance rendered upon many occasions.

HILDA GAMLIN.

CAMDEN LAWN,
  BIRKENHEAD, 1892.

CONTENTS.

CHAPTER I.

CHAPTER XIII.

CHAPTER XIV.

CHAPTER XV.

ILLUSTRATIONS.

MEMORIES OR CHRONICLES
OF
BIRKENHEAD.

CHAPTER I.

INTRODUCTORY—THE OLD GRANGE FARM AND ITS TENANTS.

IT is the fashion now-a-days for everyone who can and can't write, to jot down their memoirs. Everyday life has its bright phases, and a fund of amusement can be extracted from our surroundings if we only " make a note " of them, and book the best (or the worst) of the incidents which cross our path. The thing that has passed for ever beyond reach is clothed in a halo of sanctity that never enveloped it during existence. Thus we speak of the " good old times," and honour them as we shall in turn be honoured by the people as yet unborn. We little appreciate our own generation, yet those who will take our vacant places will speak of our day as of a good thing that has vanished.

The tales I purpose telling are half a lifetime back, and may prove interesting to the new comers who occupy the old homesteads and more modern erections. I could have wished that an abler pen had undertaken the task, but, *faut de mieux*, I offer my humble exposition, and to the critic who shall find fault, I simply say, " Do better." To account for my presumption in framing these memories of ancient days, let me state that I was born on Grange Mount,

in a year that I intend to keep to myself, but I often
feel thankful that I am not of sufficient importance to
receive the public reminder that I am older than I
wish to be, or the church bells ring a merry peal to
rejoice that I am getting on in life! Suffice it to say
that I am one of the old stock who associated with the
first inhabitants of this once rural spot, and from their
companionship were extracted the descriptions which
I am thus enabled to record. No attempt has been
made at literary finish, trusting that readers will
prefer the anecdotes in their true and natural state;
and I have written in the first person, finding it so
much easier thus to express myself.

In the early days of Birkenhead, its people were
in a fair way to make a historical name for themselves by patient, quiet plodding; the town gradually
rose and enlarged, and small fortunes were realised
within its boundaries. But a wicked prophet arose,
and blasted our even course by forecasting us as the
" City of the Future." Pride comes before a fall!
From that day forth commenced our sliding scale of
decline. Relying on the seer's prediction that we were
to be great among men, we contented ourselves with
vaunting our prospective grandeur, and stayed the
hand that should have steered us to prosperity,
while the prophet laughed merrily in his corner at our
misinterpretation of his prevision, for "the future"
never arrives!

In that happy time of the town's infancy its
inmates lived in pleasant accord as one united family,
rejoicing in each other's success, and co-operating in
business advancement; but with the downfall of the
embryo city entered the demons of discord, " social
distinction," rivalry, and kindred elements of mortal

weakness that undermine every prosperous constitution.   As the face of nature changed, so likewise were the dwellers thereon transformed, and the few remnants of those halcyon days will shake their heads, and regretfully tell you, " There are none like the old people."

I purpose to intermingle the outlines of landmarks that have disappeared with recollections of those who peopled the land of the past, and start with the almost forgotten old Grange Farm.   When it existed it had for its boundaries what are now known as Alfred Road, Grange Mount, Euston Grove, and Euston Place.   The entrance to the homestead was in the middle of Alfred Road.   A narrow flight of steps and long straight walk, dividing the old-fashioned country garden, led to the porch, on either side of which grew an immense sweetbriar bush that shed sweetness afar, and just within the door stood that relic of ancient days, "grandfather's clock."   The boughs in the orchard were gorgeous with their blaze of blossom ; some of the apple and plum trees and currant bushes still flourish in their original places in the gardens of the modern villas erected on the old Grange land. The privet hedge which forms their margin is the same that bounded the farm ; the outbuildings were entered from the corner of Alfred Road and Grange Mount ; the old barn remained on that spot for some years after the rest was dismantled.

About the year 1846 the farm was in the occupation of a couple named Davies, thoroughly countrified and worthy people, the old lady an exceedingly kind neighbour to my mother, sending her jugs of cream and pats of sweet butter to grace the table when she knew that a friend was expected.   One afternoon she gathered a spray of her lovely damask roses, and, holding it to be inhaled, she remarked, "Wouldn't it look pratty in a bonnet?" She had an impediment in her speech. My mother once told her that she had engaged a new housemaid, on which Mrs. Davies expressed her good wishes that the stranger might be all that could be desired, in these words, "Well, I hope she'll shoot (suit) you." On one of the stones in the wall which enclosed an opposite field, the old man carved the initials of himself and wife, $T_D{}^A$ (Thomas and Anne Davies), with some date early in this century beneath.

The Grange Farm passed into one or two strange hands of little moment until the family of Mr. E. entered possession. This gentleman considerably increased and monopolised the cab traffic. Little respect had he for those who are styled "carriage people," and still less for those who did not patronise him. On the evenings when an assembly would be held at the Music Hall, his portly figure invariably stood at the exit to guard the interests of his regular customers, and secure them comfortable conveyance to their homes. One night, after a grand concert, he occupied his usual station. A gentleman who harnessed a couple of horses to his equipage, said, in his pompous little voice, "Ah, E. E., get me a car."* He received the query as to how he came down to the hall. "Oh, my carriage brought me down." "Then," said this independent minister to vehicular requirements, "let your carriage take you back again."

* Public conveyances were called "cars" in those days.

CHAPTER II.

The Happy Valley—Westbourne Road and the Ghost of the Hollows—Hamilton Square— Albert Smith visits Birkenhead—Old Bidston Hall—The Lighthouse.

The most rural spot in the locality was known as " The Happy Valley," in Tranmere Vale. The name meant all it suggests, a lovely vale with primroses covering the banks, the wild violets and woodbine so profuse that a stroll in the early dewy morning enabled one to secure a graceful decoration for the breakfast table. Honey-suckle, wild roses and blackberries followed in seasonable succession. I made a beautiful and varied collection of butterflies, captured among the thistles which thickly abounded. What a lovely rendezvous wherein to picnic; wild flowers to collect, birds' nests to seek, mushrooms to gather. At this period the sole dwelling houses were eight villas, the locality which is sadly deteriorated, is now covered with the lowest class of tenement, leaving no trace of the sylvan glade. On a visit lately paid to one of the villas, the cocks and hens received me in the parlour ! A running stream (which went by the name of " the Rubicon " at this point) meandered along the exact course now known as " the Borough Road," until it reached the vicinity of the Central Station of to-day; here its dimensions increased to proportions that per- mitted a pleasure boat to move at ease, and gave its name to the adjacent row of cottages (Pool Terrace) now demolished in order to enlarge the roadway.

In the far-away past, an open sewer or ditch chased its uneven course along what is now called " Westbourne Road." An irregular beaten track was the only pathway, and it was no unusual thing for the unwary pedestrian to find his foot submerged in the black slime. When streets were christened, a finger post was erected by our governing powers, the Commissioners. It was placed on the border of Grange Lane* pointing upwards to the murky swamp, and thereon, under the direction of a wicked wit, was painted the covert significant landmark, " Water Street," an appellation it bore for one day only, as my father, who then resided at the top of this silent stream, had it erased and replaced by " Westbourne Road," a name it still bears. I well remember seeing the first cab go down that way which was literally " no road." I watched with the fascination with which one anticipates a catastrophe, and the fact that its dissection did not take place *en route* ought to have served its builder as a testimonial. In the immediate vicinity (Cole Sreet) my father was actually upset owing to the bad road, and, though he escaped with a shaking, the driver was seriously hurt, but this rather anticipates, for in our primitive days no cabs for hire were obtainable, and when one solitary vehicle was started as an enterprise, its use had to be bespoken.

When all around were fields, divided by hedges, broken in places by the depredations of blackberry gatherers, there lay in the centre between Westbourne and Oxton Roads two pits called " the Hollows," and thereabouts walked the ghost whom

* Now Grange Road West.

nobody ever saw, but such faith was there in its existence, that if your washerwoman lived on the other
side of you and the ghost, you need never expect your
laundry if the shades of night had advanced. The old
name in Wirral for an unearthly visitant was a
" buggon," and one who attached himself to Prenton
is commemorated, as is usual with such weird subjects,
in rhyme:—

> " When gorse is in blossom and holly is green,
> Prenton Hall buggon is then to be seen."

The house which the family of " Laird " has made
famous in Hamilton Square was formerly a boarding
school for young ladies, and the proprietresses,
" Misses Bisset and Hamilton." My mother was a
pupil. It will scarcely be credited, yet such is a
fact, for so few houses stood in the days of which I
write, that one morning my mother was using a field
glass in her house on the top of Grange Mount for
the purpose of looking for the carriages containing a
wedding party from Hamilton Square, when she detected my father approaching the Square, recognising
him by the fashionable white trousers he had on.
Another family living in Belmont Terrace, Oxton
Road, used to watch for the master's return. On his
appearance in Hamilton Street they began to lay the
cloth. The block of buildings in the Square was
not all erected at the same time, and Mortimer
and Brandon Streets were divided by a large delph,
surmounted with the permissive intimation—" Rubbish may be shot here." Availing themselves of
this privilege, the sweeps materially assisted in
making ground by depositing therein the contents of
their bags. Things invariably go from one extreme to

the other, and eventually our municipal palace was reared on a foundation that any one who was so minded could contribute to.

In the wide area of country, the districts formerly were very scattered, Albert Smith, the pioneer of panoramas, could tell his experience of his search for St. Michael's Terrace, in Oliver Street. None could direct him to its whereabouts; he was referred by the market authorities to the parish offices, and concluded his adventures by passing over the planks of some unfinished houses which collapsed and carried him with them. He did not foresee a great future for the place, and was perhaps the exception which is necessary to prove the rule. However, he had one gratifying recollection of the neighbourhood, the "Ham and Egg Shop," in Old Bidston Village, in reality the village inn, "The Ring o'Bells," which obtained its notoriety from the tasty manner in which the ham and eggs were served. Albert Smith's grateful recollections prompted him to introduce the house into his amusing tale, "Christopher Tadpole." I remember him, with his pleasant face and bushy red beard, holding up a pair of tiny shoes, baby size, which he assured his audience assembled at his panorama—"The Overland Route to China"—he had actually seen upon the feet of a Chinese lady.

Bidston has every semblance of age. Not the least interesting is the old windmill on the hill, rapidly falling to decay, but still a beautiful landmark, calling up associations of past labour that preceded machinery. The view from this eminence is very extended, and many a gorgeous sunset has been watched in an evening by those who now sleep in God's acre at the foot of the hill.

Photographed by E. Morris, 97 Price Street.

THE OLD WINDMILL AT BIDSTON.

The Old Hall at Bidston has its legend of the gambler's luck, that by a bottle of wine it passed into the hands of a stranger, and by a bottle of wine the original owner obtained repossession. The record of the coincidence is preserved in two carved stone decanters surmounting the well-preserved arched gateway leading to the house, while another symbolic trace of the tastes and proclivities of its former owners was a summer-house in the form of the ace of clubs.

The Duke of Monmouth is said to have met his co-conspirators in a summer-house at the foot of Bidston Hill—this may be the one referred to.

The Hall was built by the sixth Earl of Derby as a summer residence; it was formerly a goodly demesne and park. The eighth Earl of Derby lived here in privacy in embarrassed circumstances, owing to his father's resistance to the Parliamentary forces; Lathom Hall and Knowsley being almost destroyed in the conflict.

Bidston Lighthouse was built in 1771 to replace the one washed away at Leasowe. Considering the importance of the present lighthouse, it is interesting to note that 100 years prior to the erection of the first one, the Mayor and Burgesses of Liverpool petitioned against lighthouses, averring they would prove hurtful to mariners, and entrap them into danger if they relied on them. But the district bore a very bad character when those good men petitioned to protect the seamen's lives. Smugglers and wreckers tenanted the farms, so as to carry on their nefarious trade, and many a vessel had been lured to doom by the false lights they displayed. Before telegraph service came into use, leading Liverpool merchants had their own private flag-poles at Bidston. When any of their vessels were seen in the offing, the owners were signalled by running up a flag which could be seen at Liverpool.

CHAPTER III.

All Hands to the Pump—Wellington Terrace—
Small Beginnings have Great Endings—The
Omen Fulfilled—Mrs. B's Little Tea—The
Market.

THE first absolute Welsh resident in Birkenhead
settled in a pretty cottage somewhere in the vicinity
of the present Town Station. The good lady could
hardly speak a word of English, and had brought
with her her tall Welsh hat. A Mr. Pim set up a
kiln for the manufacture of bricks in Claughton Road.
Everybody was greatly alarmed on the first night of
its being aglow, and one and all (native police
included) ran in the direction of the kiln with buckets
of water to extinguish the fire, the fire engine hurrying
up with all speed also. Not long after this episode
the Welsh lady was summoned to account for her own
chimney being on fire. Growing irate on finding
herself in what she considered an ignominious position, the kind-hearted magistrate said, soothingly,
" Well, Mrs. ——, I suppose it was not a very big
fire? " To which she rejoined in a fretful tone, in
broken English, " It's no so big as Pim kiln brick,"
for she thought it inconsistent to call her up for her
miniature flare-up while the big kiln fumed away.

A private toll-gate barred the way at the top of
Clifton Park,* and adjoining the well-known boot

* Now Clifton Road.

shop of Messrs. Brown & Nicholson, one of the oldest
establishments in the district, having held its ground
for forty years.

A retired sea captain built himself a house on the
summit of Clifton Park. In his garden he planted
a pear tree, which he called "the tenant's pear
tree," and every Sunday afternoon, while it bore
fruit, he generously contributed about a dozen small
pears to assist the dessert of his tenants in Wellington Terrace. Those old-fashioned villas look
as if they could tell old-fashioned tales. A rising man
once occupied one of those tenements, and a successful speculation justified his calling together his
friends to rejoice with him. As the guests filed in to
supper, it was observed that, in order to ensure a good
"fizz," the champagne was placed inside the fender,
close to the fire. A subdued whisper told him that
it was customary to surround champagne with ice,
and it was removed. They say we learn something new every day, and *he* learnt something that
day. He lived to preside over many a sumptuous
repast. I wonder if he ever gave a thought to his first
party; but they were a merry band withal!

There were so few in Birkenhead about the year
1849 that everybody knew everybody, and the ladies
took a hand at whist in an evening as well as the
gentlemen. Certain houses, mostly in Wellington
Terrace, had their appointed nights for the reception
of friends. It was unanimously arranged that the
visitors were to take "pot-luck," and no expense was
to be incurred for supper; whatever cold meat the
larder contained was to satisfy all needs. This plan
lasted some little time, and worked well, but the
mischievous spirit of rivalry crept in, and undermined

those sociable gatherings. One would furnish a hot steak, another advanced to chickens; one would not be outdone by the other, until these oft-repeated suppers became burdens to bear.

Meanwhile, a cloud of another nature was gathering into a storm, which in due time burst. At first the ladies played for trifling amounts, just to lend interest to the recreation. The stakes gradually increased until they assumed the proportions of little piles of gold. In the midst of a game a lady, the one who could best meet a loss, threw down her cards, and incurred the displeasure of her husband by refusing to play any more, on the grounds that some of the ladies who were at table could not afford to lose the high stakes, and she would not countenance their risk. One of these female speculators invariably cried from mortification whenever her luck reduced her hoard.

A supper party was convened at the house of a lady who loved a lord. The meeting was summoned to do honour to Mr. (afterwards Sir) W. J. It happened that this gentleman's engagements prevented his attendance after he and all guests had accepted invitations, and part of the repast was prepared. The supper without the magnate was not to be thought of, and it was postponed for a couple of nights to suit his convenience. As the guests seated themselves, the edibles presented the most flabby and uninviting appearance (oysters might be particularised). The pheasants which were laid before the great guest had exceeded even the orthodox state of decay, and as he placed the fork in one of the birds preparatory to dissection, a wicked look was in his eye as he said to his special friend, with much point, " V., shall I give you a little GAME?" On these minor deficiencies the hostess beamed her eternal smile of self-satisfaction. Her refreshment department frequently included varieties seen nowhere else, such as wax fruit in lieu of the more perishable article. The host of the stale entertainment was once sadly affected by sea-sickness on his passage between Calais and Dover, and during one of his convulsions, he made an involuntary offering to Father Neptune of his false teeth.

A year or two later, the above-mentioned Mr. V. was dining at a friend's house on Grange Mount. Before taking seats it was noticed that the guests numbered the ominous thirteen, and someone was sent for to break the spell. Mr. V. turned to his neighbour, saying, " As if the Almighty would make use of so insignificant a circumstance to call one of his creatures to himself." Before the anniversary of that day came round, the speaker had answered the call.

In the days when friendly intercourse aimed no higher than pleasant little teas that vividly recall Mrs. Gaskell's pretty country tales, an old lady residing in Kenyon Terrace invited a few of her intimates to spend the evening with her. Her husband, a nice, harmless old man, had a liking for strong waters, and sometimes bore signs of the extent of his affection, and perhaps his wife made more of it than she need have done; but on this special occasion she induced him to retire for the night before her guests arrived, and some little apology was made for his absence. Tea was over, and a pleasant buzz of conversation prevailed, when the handle of the door turned, and in crept the old gentleman with a smile on his face just like a naughty child that had got up on hearing there was company. There he stood in the doorway, looking so quiet and guilty. Then up spake his wife, and she meant what she said: "Go to bed, Mr. B.; go to bed." Poor old fellow; he just gave one look as if he would like to stay with us, and away he went. We really felt inclined to ask if he might stop up.

On a Saturday morning, at market, this old lady might be relied upon for the most recent gossip, and sometimes she anticipated events. If the blinds were down in any house where sickness was known to prevail, she required no further intimation to circulate that it was a house of mourning, and some are still walking and talking whom she committed to an early death many a year ago.

The market was always a pleasant *rendezvous* for the ladies bent on housekeeping forage. The fountains in the principal avenue, with the four stone lions at the base, cast up their refreshing spray, which fell into the basin below, cool and soothing. These ornaments were removed, as obstructions to traffic. Alas, there is plenty of room for them now! One morning my mother was buying me a toy at one of the stalls, when a plain little body in a long cloak came up to have a chat, and thus addressed her: "Buying 'tyes;' you're always buying 'tyes;' when 'Lizbeth was little, she'd only two 'tyes.'" Now 'Lizbeth was of high degree, and you never would have thought that this humble woman was the mother of a lady of title!

A little dwarf kept an egg stall in the market. To increase his height he wore a very high top hat. His wife was a massive woman, and once she tried to evade the ferry toll by carrying him in her apron. The ferry officials being too desirous to inspect the bulky parcel, caused the dwarf to reveal his identity in an outburst of bad language.

The market place which preceded the present one was a partially-covered area adjoining the old and now dismantled Town Hall. On the open part of this area there was roasted an ox, in the year 1837, to celebrate the coronation of the young Queen Victoria.

WOODSIDE FERRY IN 1818.

CHAPTER IV.

THE DOCKS AND THE HISTORICAL BANNER—WOOD-
SIDE FERRY—QUEEN VICTORIA ON THE MERSEY—
THE DEATH OF MR. C. ENFORCES A WISE LAW—
MAY DAY REVELS—THE PRIMITIVE POST OFFICE—
HOLT HILL.

THE laying of the foundation stone of the docks by
Sir Philip Egerton was a scene of gay life that could
hardly be surpassed. Though it was October 23,
1844, the morning broke sweet and balmy as a fresh
May day. At the early hour of six, cannon boomed
an awakening summons that the great day had
dawned, and each one gleefully arose and donned his
best apparel to participate in the revelries. The
whole population of Liverpool seemed to turn out to
witness what promised to be an unparalleled display.
The Woodside ferry boats, decked with streamers and
evergreens, conveyed the multitude across the river
with the utmost expedition, and as they neared the
Cheshire shore the clang of merry Church bells pealed
a token of great rejoicing, and the whole of the ferry
slip was encircled with flags suspended from an
immense height. All the vessels at anchor near
Woodside honoured the festival by decorating their
masts with flags, and cannon kept up a continuous
roar. Flags and evergreens crossed the streets of the
route of the procession, and on one corner of Hamilton
Square triumphal arches of laurel were erected. The

procession included trumpeters on horseback, the Champion dressed in armour as Seneschal of the Priory of Birkenhead. He bore a shield, and his glittering apparel of bright polished steel glistened in the sun, he carried the pennon of the Prior on his lance—the whole costume was copied from one of the old stained glass windows of the Priory. Then followed fire engines, some with postillions, others with firemen in uniform. A printing press sent forth an ode among the crowd commemorative of the occasion. Numerous friendly lodges walked, separated by splendid bands of music. Messrs. Laird's men carried iron models of ships. Sawyers had grotesque figures pretending to saw, &c. From first to last 16,000 persons are said to have taken part in the show, which took three quarters of an hour in passing through the Square. In order to give general pleasure to the poorer inhabitants, a meeting of local gentry had been convened at which the sum of £2,000 was handsomely subscribed. Out of this fund they were enabled to pay each workman or labourer a day's wages, and though general holiday was held no one suffered loss thereby. Bread and meat were bountifully distributed, and school children were supplied with buns and fruit.

The Docks and Park were formally opened by Lord Morpeth, on Easter Monday, April 5, 1847, With the influx of workmen necessary to carry out the gigantic operations, prosperity reigned in the town, money rapidly circulated, and as an instance it may be told that an apparently small shopkeeper in Watson Street was nightly heard counting his gold accruing from sales to the sons of toil. Who shall despise the men of labour? Their income brought luck and life, and when the mighty work was accomplished, the workers went to execute a distant contract, and the place has never looked up since their departure.

When the foundation stone of the Birkenhead Docks was laid, it was suggested that a graceful remembrance of the auspicious occasion which augured so well for the rising town, should be made to Sir Philip and Lady Egerton, who had taken a prominent part in the proceedings, and the Committee decided that the gifts should consist of a pair of carriage footstools for the lady, and a representative banner for the gentleman. Birkenhead had then no coat of arms to emblazon, so the legendary squirrel, which tradition tells could once have " leapt from tree to tree, from Birkethead to Hilbree," was depicted in needlework on the banner as a memorial. The execution of the design was entrusted to a lady highly accomplished in the fashionable employment of producing pictures in fine canvas and silks, which were afterwards framed as screens. Landseer's " Bolton Abbey in Olden Times," containing the portraits of the Cavendish family of that day, and " The burying of the Scotch Regalia," were the favourite subjects. Ladies confided to this expert the filling in of the eyes of their figures. She and her two industrious daughters worked night and day upon this now historical banner, for the allotted time in which to execute it was very limited. The crowd had already assembled to see the procession when she arrived, and struggled through the dense mass of humanity bearing aloft the banner. The sum she received as remuneration was £30, every penny of which went in Doctor's fees and medical necessaries, for on her return home she found one daughter extended on the floor, and the other on the couch, with the first symptoms of brain fever developed.   They had broken down under the strain of overwork.

One calm night in April, 1814, three travellers arrived at Birkenhead ferry desirous of conveyance to Liverpool, but paused appalled by the demand of the boatman, that they should fee him one guinea a-piece. So they resolved to put up for the nonce at the inn, hoping that a night's reflection would result in an abatement of the exorbitant terms of ferryage.   Daylight found them in a worse plight, as birds of passage were such a rarity, mine host presented the wayfarers with an extortionate bill, while the boatman adhered to his charge.

The first steamboat that plied between Liverpool and Birkenhead was a private speculation, which proved disastrous financially from want of public support.   When the present century had reached its thirties, the chief access to Liverpool was by a small sailing boat, which crossed the river on market days for a charge of 6d. a head to its passengers.   Living persons remember crossing by a late boat, and having to take a lantern to light their way.   A pathway through a corn-field (now Bridge Street) led to a flight of steps descending to the shore, which from New Brighton up to Eastham was one continuous line.

St. Mary's Church was erected by F. R. Price, Esq., Lord of the Manor, in accordance with a stipulation over a sale of land to Messrs. Grindrod, Hetherington & Addison, who designed to build an hotel and landing-place, and required that new streets should be cut, and a church established to popularise their own speculation.   The foundation-stone of the edifice was laid by the Right Hon. Lord Kenyon in July, 1819.   The hotel was reared by the enterprising

proprietors on the present site of Messrs. Laird's works. There were pleasure grounds in front, and a fine sloping tea garden, with rustic alcoves, bordered on the water's edge by fine old oak trees, and here, on the occasion of the visit to Liverpool of her Majesty Queen Victoria in 1851, the school-children of the various Birkenhead schools were congregated to see their Sovereign sail by in the yacht *Fairy*. On the Cheshire side the vessel was brought as close as possible to the land, and as it passed the assembled youngsters, the Queen raised up the Prince of Wales (then a little lad) and bid him raise his cap. This he did, and the elated little people who were lustily singing the National Anthem broke off abruptly and sent forth a ringing cheer with their fresh voices.

Within the memory of the present generation, donkeys plied for hire on Woodside shore, and Tranmere had its supply of bathing machines, but tanneries erected at the latter place destroyed the beauty and cleanliness of the river margin.

A well-meaning religious enthusiast took his daily station on the ten o'clock morning boat from Woodside, to remind his merchant companions, who were crossing in search of lucre, that there was a business of more import than money-making. His text was invariably the same: "What doth it profit a man to gain the whole world and lose his own soul?" He was respectfully listened to for many a day, until he found imitators of more offensive calibre, and the old gentleman was asked to discontinue his earnest homilies.

About the year 1850 it was customary for ladies to stroll each afternoon on the promenade at Woodside Ferry, which jutted out into the river, and at the end of which stood the lighthouse,* with variegated glass in the lanthorn, and near it a large bell that rung out warning during fogs. Here they watched the passengers disembark from the ferry boats *Queen*, *Prince*, *Lord Morpeth*, and *Nun*, and walk up the sloping slip to the pay gates, close to Gough's Woodside Hotel. Those were good old times for Woodside Ferry, which was spoken of as the best managed in the world, and the captains of the boats bore the highest reputation for the skill with which they controlled and guided them to their berths. The familiar figures of the ferry officials were for ever at their posts. Captain Reid under the clock, by the chains which divided the up-coming from the down-going passengers. Mr. Hughes and Mr. Sargent so courteous at the contractors' gate; old Jerry's weather-beaten face, with his "Hurry, hurry on there," just before the gangway was wheeled ashore; and the fine black dog that had saved as many lives as old Jerry. The one-armed porter with a hook attached to the maimed limb, so sharp to spy the luggage on the vehicle as it came down the hill, and the first to open the door as it stopped. On the top of the steps, outside the pay-gates, sat the meek little gingerbread woman; gentle and simple purchased her wares enveloped in blue paper; wet or dry she never was missing until she and the pay-gates went together.

During a very severe frost about forty years ago, the Woodside ferrymen received a temporary addition of 2s. 6d. to their weekly wages. As the weather moderated, it was intimated that this would be withdrawn. Two of the town officials, however, were nominated for an increase of salary to be derived from the money discontinued to the men, who accordingly

---

* Now for sale. Who ever heard of a lighthouse for sale?

organised a strike, and as each man's wages was tendered to him on next pay day, he returned it. The ferrymen thereon refused to work the boats, and for three hours there was no service between Birkenhead and Liverpool, the Commissioners wisely giving way, and yielding the concession.

In those days it was immaterial if you jumped off or on the ferry boats, or miscalculated your distance and became immersed in the water. Still, these oft-repeated mishaps so seriously delayed the passengers, while an attempt was made to deprive Neptune of his prey, that a by-law was passed, to which penalties were attached if entrance or exit were effected by any other means than the gangway. As is invariably the case whenever a wise law is laid down, there were some who would contest and defeat it. A Mr. C. was engaged as solicitor for the malcontents, and the cause was approaching its hearing when one night Mr. C. crossed from Liverpool in the twelve o'clock boat, he dozed in the cabin, and was unaware of the disembarkation of the passengers at Woodside. The vessel started to lay up in the Sloyne when one of the crew aroused the sleeper, who rushed up the cabin stairs and leaped on to the landing stage. He caught the chains, which rebounded more than he had calculated upon. He lost his balance, and fell into the river. A swift-flowing incoming tide bore him rapidly out of sight, and help never reached him. A month afterwards a gamekeeper found his remains on the shore at Eastham, the watch upon him, the gift of a friend, being the only clue to his identity. The legal contest was never fought, for this painful episode would have been evidence for the defence.

The day that ushered in the merry month of May

was an ever-memorable one in the forties, for a miniature carnival brought together a large concourse of sight-seers. Those who took part in the display assembled in a field in Abbey Street, whereon justice now asserts her rights against county offenders against the laws. Men garbed themselves as women in showy chintz skirts, with polonaise-shaped tops, looped up. Their heads were encased in the cap which at that period was generally worn by females, the front of which was net, deftly quilled. The whiskers of the mummers projecting beyond this feminine adorn-ment, had a very laughable effect. No one wore moustaches in those days; they were a fashion to come.

The May Queen was represented by one of the sterner sex, crowned with floral monstrosities that would have made the fortune of a horticulturist if he could have coaxed nature to copy them. Gigantic *blue* roses mingled with white, yellow, and pink, and an enormous bunch of many-hued ribbons dangled from the back of his head. Festoons of gaudy ribbons and flowers decorated the skirt. The band that accompanied the show was composed of a kettle-drum, tin whistles and little rattles, and small trays did for tambourines. With a capering step, and practising many giddy pranks in their progress, such as kissing women, etc., they went down Chester Street, past the old ferry pay-gates, by the Woodside Hotel, and up Hamilton Street, until they reached the green pastures, now Hinson Street. Here the Maypole was erected, streamers of ribbon floating gaily at the top. As the revellers advanced, a really graceful mazy dance was performed at intervals. On arriving at this point in Hamilton Street a collection was made

from the lookers-on, and then there issued from the
May ground the female element, who now took part in
the show, their dresses pretty short, chemisette bodices,
and the sleeves turned up, leaving the arms bare.
The men faced the women, and they advanced
towards each other in threes, forming into straight
rows of nine in each line; then, with a step partly
swaying, partly capering, they met and took partners,
dancing off to the field, where the first who entered
encircled the Maypole with his arm and swung round
it, the rest following in like manner. Then all joined
hands, and gambolled in an immense circle round the
pole in true Old English style. On one of these
festivals, just in the height of the fun, they were met
in Hamilton Street by a lady who was wending her
way to Hamilton Square, then the abode of local
aristocracy. Dressed in the ungainly crinoline, and
sack jacket with large bell sleeves, her face hidden in
her coal scuttle bonnet, she feared them not, nor fled,
as one more prudent might have done, for on that day
no one escaped their attentions. She pursued her
course with mincing step, holding up her dress with
both hands, at each side. One lively dancer bounded
in front of her, holding out his own skirts to mimic
her. She merely gave him a contemptuous look, and
steadily proceeded, whereon her tormentor put his face
under her bonnet, and tried to kiss her. Up went her
hand, and he received a resounding slap on the cheek.
Resuming her conceited, old-fashioned walk, she continued without further molestation, while her per-
secutor tried to turn sober earnest into a joke, by
rubbing his bruised cheek as if hurt, and the crowd
cheered—whom it would be hard to say, but it is more
than probable that the lady had *not* their sympathy.

Foolery, foolery, but alack for the days that have gone!

The first post office in Birkenhead was in Chester Street, close to the ferry, and you made your applications or received impertinence through a small sliding window, that could be opened or shut at will, and it was no unusual occurrence for an interview to come to an abrupt termination by this barrier cutting off communication. The front room was retained for her Majesty's service, and in the back apartment would be displayed a joint of uncooked meat and a ham, for its proprietor combined the boarding-house on a very small scale with his higher postal duties. Later, the adjoining front window was taken on behalf of her Majesty, and the meat asserted itself to the fore instead of the rear. A relic of bygone customs is to be found in this neighbourhood. " The stocks," where formerly the culprit sat in enforced detention to receive the jeers of his fellowmen, were inserted in the boundary wall of St. Mary's Church, on the corner of Abbey and Church Streets, a projecting stone of which remains to this day.

On the right hand of the road from Tranmere Ferry, leading to Holt Hill, and at the foot of the hill itself, once stood a miniature inn, whitewashed, and with green-painted shutters to the windows. Up aloft there hung a diminutive green gate, surmounted by this inscription :—

> This gate hangs well, it hinders none;
> Refresh and pay, and travel on.

A little further up the incline, in a tiny house called " Hillside Cottage," there resided a lady who possessed the rare accomplishment of playing tunes on

a Jew's harp. On the summit of this rise stands the
" Bay House," built to represent amidships of a vessel.
The entrance of the opposite dwelling-house was
effected by passing under the jaw-bones of a whale.
In the time of civil war the army of Cromwell was
called upon to halt upon this eminence ; the name
" The Holt," which it now bears, is a corruption of
the word "halt." From this vantage ground the hand
that destroyed so many beauteous architectural monu-
ments, aimed its cruel weapons, and wrecked the
priory in the vale below. The Priory house was
garrisoned by Royalists and captured by Parliament-
arians in 1644.

CHAPTER V.

TRAINERS OF MANNERS AND MORALS—THE DOCTOR'S
LECTURE—OUR POET AND WOMAN OF GENIUS—
EXILED FOREIGN NOBILITY—COMPETITION EXTRA-
ORDINARY—UNINVITED GUESTS.

FOREMOST among the directors of youthful intellect
who settled in Claughton, at Claughton Cottage,
Slatey Road, * (then Slatey Lane) was a bright elderly
lady, very small, but sharp as a needle. Her ringlets
shook like merry little bells round her clever little
head. While engaged in teaching she was likewise
occupied in making wax flowers, which accomplishment in her hands compared most favourably with
nature. Her pupils were but wee things. One afternoon the old lady told each of them to write her a
letter, and this is what one of them wrote: " It is your
birthday to-morrow; please how old are you? "

A learned and reverend doctor once arrived in the
town, and opened an academy as a trainer of youthful
scions in knowledge and morals. His previous educational establishment had collapsed from monetary
deficiencies, and some thought the catastrophe might
have been averted. Being somewhat of an orator, he
was invited to lecture to the boys on the reformatory
ship *Akbar.* The proverbial text which he selected

* Now the studio of that excellent photographer, Mr. W.
Clement Lavis.

for his discourse was remarkable under the circumstances; he feelingly and emphatically impressed upon the lads that "honesty is the best policy!" At the commencement of one of the quarters into which the educational year was then divided, he took a few of the new pupils down to New Brighton, and there occurred a scene of which Charles Dickens would have made the most. He walked up and down the Promenade with his young companions, with whom he was evidently upon the most fatherly of terms. After taking a few turns they all entered the refreshment rooms; an inspection through one of the windows showed that he had condescended to accept a glass of ale from one of his pupils. The scene was rich—the importance of the boy in Eton jacket and top hat, as he opened his little purse to pay for his master's treat; and the benevolent benignity which beamed on the pedagogue's rubicund face as he swallowed the lad's pocket money. He was a good father in his own family circle, and never set any difficulties in the way of his daughters marrying his best pupils, while he gave them as *dot* that invaluable gift, "the parental blessing."

We have had our poet. but a poet is mostly a pest; he is one of the genus who has to go from home to be appreciated. Ask him to recite in the midst of a party that has reached a point of thorough enjoyment, and a damp depression immediately envelopes the company, which only the activity of an uncommonly good hostess can disperse. I have him before me now, oblivious to the fact that hearers are stealing noiselessly from the room, while flows along in seraphic ecstasy his " Thou of my thou," (with action). The only person who ever gave him an attentive ear was a lady who had lost her love at sea. For many a day after he had gone down into the depths, she wrote him refrains of fidelity, sealed them with wax and kisses, and cast them into the outflowing tide of the Mersey at New Brighton. Nightly, the poet was to be found sitting lowly at her feet, as a poet should, while he poured out his inane effusions, and thus two, whom society could well spare, found solace in each other's company.

We had our woman of genius likewise, but she did not add one iota to our lustre, for she daily reposed on her couch shoeless, with nature contending to make herself evident in a very decided manner through her stockings, while her children grew around her in absolute neglect, and the albums were full of the thanks of editors. If she went out, she slithered (excuse the word, but it is so expressive of that march of intellect) along in heel-trodden slippers, and her gold chain hung as far down her back as in front of her.

We had our exiled foreign nobility—two Polish Counts, not of much account. Count K., a dark little man with a villainous leer—*on dit* said he was "the servant's lover," but the gentlemen knew more about him than the ladies, for he was only tolerated at card parties. The other, Count O., was of higher caste, a quiet looking elderly gentleman in a grey suit of clothes, but he found his troubles surpass his endurance, and the dawn of one morning disclosed him suspended, Judas-like, from the branch of a decayed tree.

There were two inseparables of yore, prominent figures on the cricket ground, popular, noisy and good-hearted, yet possessing the one alloy that is said to mar everything pleasant, which in their case was disease of ravenous appetites, and at each hospitable table to which they were invited, the one vied with the other as to which could despatch the most. It will be admitted that these were unenviable qualifications for society. One evening they called upon a gentleman, and were shown into the dining-room; on the table reposed a handsome cake, intended to figure at the next day's festival, the christening of the youngest born of the house. Before the owner of the cake appeared, these two gourmands attacked and demolished it; a feat the proprietor never forgave. Nor was this the only escapade committed by these "villainous appetites." Strolling one evening on Oxton Common, they found a door ajar, and the cottager's wife, absent while the cakes toasted before the fire. If any fugitive king had been left in charge he was absent in body as well as in mind, and the invaders partook of the humble feast, and beat dishonourable retreat. History sayeth not that they left any visible traces of their visit to recoup the lowly dame, the evident testimony of their raid was invisible !

CHAPTER VI.

The Park—Easter Egg Festival—The Invasion
of Swindlers—A Word to the Wise—Leamington Diamonds—The Travelling Trader asks
for the Master.

When the introduction of steamboats made access
to Birkenhead easy, business men from Liverpool
brought over their families to reside. The healthy
Cheshire folk had always maintained a reputation for
hardihood, as the following extract from *The Vale
Royal of England* will testify :—" The ayr is very whole-
some, insomuch that the people of the Countrey are
seldom infected with Deseasis or Sicknesse, neither
do they use the help of the Physicians nothing so
much, as in other countries. For when any of them
are sick they make him a posset, and tye a kerchieff
on his head ; and if that will not mend him, then God
be merciful to him ! The people there live till they
are very old, some are Grandfathers their Fathers yet
living, and some are Grandfathers, before they are
married."

As the town increased its population a park was
laid out as a resort of recreation, under the designs of
the late Sir Joseph Paxton. It is considered the most
beautiful model park in the United Kingdom, and
now, when the saplings which he placed have grown
to maturity, his conception must have exceeded his
most sanguine expectations. Its principal entrance is

by a noble gateway, consisting of a central and two
side arches in the Ionic style, in imitation of the Arc
de Triomphe at Paris, and the Temple of Illyssus at
Athens, from the plans of a local architect, Mr. Lewis
Hornblower, for I write of the good old days when
the township did not consider it necessary to import
its talent, but gave the natives a chance of displaying
their capabilities. That the trust was not belied we
have ample evidence; and genius in every sphere still

Photographed by E. Morris 97 Price Street.

THE GRAND ENTRANCE TO BIRKENHEAD PARK.

abounds among us; and that it is not brought forward
to do service and credit to the town is to the discredit
of the powers who take boat and rail with their
patronage. What town can be prosperous unless all
its members work in a circle, and combine to circulate
the money among their own community? The effort
would redound to their own aggrandisement, for it
would elevate the *status* of Birkenhead, and bar the
flitting of every man of worth.

To return to the Park, which is divided into two sections, upper and lower, and covers about one hundred and eighty acres, each section having its artificial lake, well stocked with fish and aquatic wild fowl of different countries. The winding walks of three miles' length, miniature bridges, and aged trees of various hues, in some aspects are truly sylvan. Here and there the prolific lilacs, laburnums, red and white hawthorns, snowballs, and copper beeches are reflected in nature's mirror, the waters of the lakes; and the myriads of daisies in their rich profusion look like a bleaching-ground; yet not so many years ago the whole was nothing but a few uninteresting fields.

Photographed by E. Morris, 97 Price Street.

THE TEMPLE AND SWISS BRIDGE IN BIRKENHEAD PARK.

The temple-shaped erection, now used as a boat-house, was designed originally for the accommodation of a band, but was never used for that purpose. Sweet melodies issuing from that romantic spot would lend enchantment to a stroll among the fairy-like effects seen from certain points. How little we make of our opportunities. What small cost could give great pleasure!

Formerly the grounds were embellished with statues on loan, but they were ultimately recalled to adorn the estate of the owner. At the end of the lower lake reposed one of these pieces of statuary, surrounded by shrubbery. It represented the death of Alexander, which was caused by his horse Bucephalus falling upon him. This work always had its little crowd of admirers. The Park gates are of wrought iron, and contain the arms of the ancient Benedictine priory.

For some years after the Park was laid out, there were several grassy mounds inside the railings, in Ashville Road, which went by the name of "The Bonks." It would puzzle a philologist to explain the origin of the word, but such it was, and here, on every Easter Monday, children would bring baskets of coloured eggs, the one who showed the largest quantity and best assortment receiving a prize. Then a game was played. First, wickets were fixed at intervals at the foot of the "Bonks;" then the children took their eggs to the top of the hills and rolled them down, aiming to pass them unbroken between the wickets. The two who displayed the most skill won awards. A large crowd of people always assembled to witness these sports, which included the "Easter Egg dance," executed by the young people, who were then regaled on buns. These hillocks proved such a popular playground that the grass was destroyed. The eminences, thus deprived of natural growth, became unsightly, and were levelled in consequence.

Then the swindler invaded the first settlers, trusting to find, and proving them to be as green as the fields that surrounded them. The soap that had been sunk in a flat, and rendered useless for washing purposes, found its ready purchaser; the respectable young man with the lavender water at two shillings and sixpence the bottle; and the interesting account of the acres of lavender owned by his uncle at Mitcham,* in Surrey. He was past recall when it was discovered that his relative's plantations must have yielded a large percentage of dew; for after the two drops of oil of lavender which floated on the surface were absorbed in the first pocket-handkerchief, the remainder of the contents of the two bottles he had successfully planted, were proved by the analyst to be water in its purest state !

And that other young man, with his spotless white apron, and silver-bladed knife for you to try the potted shrimps and lobster before you bought his wares. Who could mistrust such evidence of honest value? Who would disfigure the pots? No, they were purchased intact; the insertion of the knife at the family repast caused their instantaneous removal from the room. This merchant disposed of all his highly-scented dainties, and on the following day we heard of him endeavouring to lay in material for his next enterprise in the shape of rotten eggs and bad pickles.

The sailor with his Japanese silks effected a sale, and he was far on his way to foreign shores to renew his stock before it transpired that each length was one yard deficient in measurement.

It is so much pleasanter to learn wisdom by the

* Mitcham, noted for its lavender fields.

experience of others than by our own, and with such examples preceding me, I have been able to withstand soap and other attractions, but I have fallen a victim to tea! A young gentleman presented himself, saying he had sailed on the seas to China, and wishful to do a little trade, he had brought home some tea to sell, and his uncle, Mr. ——, thought I might take some. I did not know his uncle (and have never been able to trace him), but I was willing to encourage the young trader in his laudable efforts to do a little for himself. So I relieved him of two pounds at two shillings and sixpence per pound. He was most desirous to supply me with double the quantity, but I declined the extra, and for my money received a printed receipt which he tore out of a book in a business-like manner. Alas! that tea had cheered someone else's table before it disgraced mine.

In my very young days, just when I was entering society, and had much to learn, I went to visit a relative in London. One day this lady presented me with a box full of what closely resembled Jersey gravel, telling me they were " Leamington diamonds" that her husband had collected when they were in residence there. He had taken them to one of the local shops, where the tradesman had sorted his gatherings, and thrown out the refuse, leaving only the gems which she munificently bestowed on me, not caring herself to go to the expense of cutting. I had visions of rings, lockets, crosses, and even a coronet, for there were ample stones to supply any amount of personal adornment; and off I went with my treasures to consult a Regent Street jeweller. Though so many years ago, how well I remember the shop with its " *Ici on parle Français,*

Espagnol," and the language of other countries, on the door as I entered. A courteous, white-haired old gentleman waited upon me. I asked the cost of cutting and setting a ring, at the same time displaying my precious stones. He took the box in his hand, examined it for a second, and then looked sharply in the direction of my bumps of sanity. He asked me how I got them, and I honestly told him, whereon he gave me this unpalatable advice: "Go and throw them away in the street; there are no diamonds there." "Oh, but there are," said I, wishful to teach him his trade. He cracked one or two to convince me, and then, while we both laughed, he kindly told me that it was a trick of trade in some localities to circulate that precious stones were to be found. When the rubbish picked up was taken to be cut, as much was charged for cutting as would provide a genuine stone. Another aunt had a really fine topaz set as a brooch, which she said she had discovered on the shore at Llandudno, but after my personal experience I misdoubt all waterside gems.

Our father was very reserved and quiet among us, and rarely spoke to the domestics. One evening while dining, the front door bell rang violently. The servant entered the room, saying, "A young man wishes to speak to you, sir." "Well, see what he wants." Back she came, after a consultation with the unknown. "Please, sir, he says he cannot tell his business to anyone else; he must see you." My father rose from his seat, for he was courteous, and would allow no one to wait; and when he appeared at the door, the young man unfolded a small parcel and said, "Please, sir, will you buy a comb?" A few emphatic words convinced the young trader that it was most unlikely that he would effect a sale, and his exit was rapid. Dinner was resumed, but we guessed by the working of our father's temples that he wished there had been no witness to the interview.

CHAPTER VII.

The Dentist Trades on Mythology—The See-saw
of Life Practically Illustrated—In Memory
of our Patentee.

THERE was a dentist in our young days who might
have had the monopoly of the custody of all the
masticators in the vicinity, only for the frequency
with which the housemaid's broom intercepted his
path to the detriment of his countenance. When we
made an afternoon call upon his wife in later times, he
always put in an appearance, during which the front
door bell would ring incessantly; its vibrations had
hardly ceased before the page boy would inform his
master that he was "wanted," which he acknowledged
by a slight inclination of the head, but so long as we
remained, he remained; and from these oft-repeated
occurrences we drew the very rational conclusion that
his clients were myths, and the bell rung purposely to
"make believe." His wife had her own ideas of
correcting a failing. Her servant maid had converted
some of her mistress's frivolities to her own personal
decoration. These were recovered and placed under
a glass shade in the drawing room, while Mary Anne
was tortured by hearing each successive visitor informed of her delinquencies. We saw those ribbons
twice within the interval of a fortnight. Poor Mary
Anne was not wholly demoralised, or she would have
smashed that shade.

It does seem an anomaly that the man who once

received a letter in which he was told that "nature never intended him for anything but a beast," (an expression of opinion in which most of his neighbours concurred,) should have a stained-glass window erected to his memory in his parish church. But so it is! Money can purchase many things, even the odour of sanctity!

Not so many years ago there were two brothers in Claughton who had obtained the degree that entitled them to the prefix Dr. to their surname B——. He who undertook the cure of souls was propriety personified. The other who attended the body and repaired broken limbs, was a perfect limb himself. Upon one special Sunday morning he started for a cock fight, bearing his bird in a bag. As he neared his brother's church he met the divine on his way to tell his congregation the best way to live. "Good morning," said the cleric, "where are you going?" "Going to take a man's leg off," said M.D., tapping his bag to indicate that it contained his instruments. "Poor fellow" was the sympathetic rejoinder. And immediately the cock crowed, and the brothers parted with the utmost speed, for the congregation was devoutly filing past to morning service.

Forty years ago it was written of Birkenhead that "every one who locates himself there is adventurous. Most of the inhabitants are merely trying the experiment of whether it is possible to make a living in the place. Few feel that security of position which enables a man to look beyond the care of himself and his family, hence there is little independence, little spirit, and little generosity. The manifestations of selfishness in all its unlovely phases are consequently found. This evil will be cured as the place becomes more settled, and men feel better assured of their own destiny. Fraternal charity, and a liberal spirit may then be known to a greater degree among the people of Birkenhead." The writer had keenly considered his surroundings. It is for us to ask ourselves, have things improved, and where is fraternal charity?

The business career of a Liverpool man is like life on a see-saw. "Here we go up, and here we go down." Money so easily made, and money so easily lost. One instance will serve to illustrate the many similar cases which annually happen among us. A party, employed on a ship, speculated in cotton during the American war, and made a fortune—money quickly earned as quickly dissolves—another venture caused him and his treasure to part company. In mental distress he actually tore the hair from his head. He recovered his spirits, however, and tried his luck again, and up he went with a bound that enabled him to buy an estate in Wales, and rent a mansion in Warwickshire. When his wife met you, she would affectedly mention having looked round in church on " her parishioners ; " *her* parishioners be it noted! Their wealth was so great that some heartless wit said the gentleman would be able to try each infallible remedy to renew nature's adornment of which he had deprived himself. When next they re-appeared among us the estate, to them, was nothing but a memory; the wife solicited needlework, which she executed to perfection, and the husband obtained employment at one of the Liverpool shipping sheds. Here to-day, and gone to-morrow, the house which the *parvenu* embellishes this year, is labelled "to let" in the next. Our world is a coterie of ups and downs.

The next character whom I propose to bring on

the scene was a " caution " in more ways than one, a
man who lived by his wits and his talents, and no
mistake.   What a sad trial he was to his landlords.
There was no getting any rent, nor yet transplanting
him and his movables ; he was neither to be coaxed
nor coerced.   So as a last resort the roof of his domi-
cile was removed, and it was the diurnal evening
amusement to stroll up and look at the dismantled
house.   Here the occupants remained until the elements came to the assistance of the landlord, and the
winds blew, and the rain rained, and the situation was
not pleasant, so they looked around and selected a
residence in a good position that unfortunately was
tenantless.   They asked for the key, which was in the
custody of a neighbouring shopkeeper, and without
making any enquiries as to whether their *entrée* would
be acceptable to the owner, they transferred themselves and their household gods within its precincts,
and a long, long time afterwards the proprietor was
trying to remember how many years it was since he
had received any rent for that unlucky demesne.   This
inventive genius (not the landlord) would strike at
everything as a speculation ; if he made anything out
of it, well and good, and if it failed, why, well and
good, too.   What did he care?   Once he took the
Theatre Royal, Argyle Street.   After a short run the
performers, band, chorus, supers, &c., struck, for they
could not exist upon the applause of the audience,
and they marched *en masse* to the house of the enterprising lessee, and surrounded it clamouring for their
salaries.   The besieged barricaded themselves in, and
eventually opened an upper window, out of which a
sovereign was thrown to the angry claimants.   When
divided, each one received fourpence !

He would interest you in one of his patents and get you to provide all fees while he shared all profits, and during the ripening of the venture he would make a daily call to extract a penny for his ferry or a five pound note to meet an emergency. But you could not help liking him. See him walk into some of the great London emporiums with his patents, his military appearance and assurance. He always booked an order.

Not long before he shuffled off this mortal coil he was made the subject of the following faithful sketch in a Liverpool comic paper :—

"Who does not know Fusby Vulpes, Esq.?

" Handsome, middle-aged, business-like air, but an indescribable something about him which one cannot fathom. Go where you will you are sure to drop across him, elated with the dreams of lucre which will accrue from his latest invention, Hullo! here he is! umbrella in one hand, some papers of a governmental looking blue in the other.

" ' Well Vulpes, anything fresh ?' we ask.

" ' Ha, yes, grand idea, my boy! Splendid thing! Millions in it ! ' says the subject of our sketch, and he unconsciously edges us in the direction of a bar not many miles from Harrington Street. ' I'll take a small gin and a little Khoosh bitters, dear,' and turn- ing to us he continues, ' I'm getting the model made. The corporation *must* accept it. Ah, thank you.' And he drains his appetiser ; and while we pay for it he runs on, ' Nothing like it, you know, the royalties must bring in, at least, ten thousand a year. By the way, have you dined yet? No! Ah, step this way.' And he edges us into the dining-room of the establish- ment we are in. He orders two steaks ' from the fillet you know, dear,' he says to the waitress, and continues to us, ' Yes, I'll have to spend a large sum in advertising. Of course I won't forget you, old boy. My dear, a small bottle of dry Sillery.' And so he runs on. We finish our dinner, and the bill is handed to Vulpes, he glances at it, and hands it to us. ' Correct, I think ? ' he asks. ' Yes,' say we, and hand it back again. He folds it up, straightens it again, and passes it over towards us. ' Yes, grand idea ; of course I'll let you stand in at the profits,' he exclaims, changing the conversation to his original subject. We pay the bill, rise from the table, and thinking we would like to know a *little* of the idea that is to render us independent of ephemeral literature, we ask Vulpes to enlighten us. ' No, my boy, not yet ; it's not yet patented.' And he bids us *au revoir*."

Still, when he went he was missed. No man need feel aggrieved at having an eccentric relative. Eccentrics are amusing varieties in the ring of life, and without wishing to emulate their attainments we hold in affectionate remembrance the memory of those who have caused us a laugh.

CHAPTER VIII.

Tillers of the Soil.—P. the Hairdresser.—Mr. Millar's Benefit Concert. — Uriah Heep in Petticoats. — The Yorkshire Schoolmaster. — The Tailor Advertises his Wrongs.

When the time arrived for the local gardens to be maintained in order, their superintendence was annually undertaken by a man named "Henry," who almost entirely monopolised their custody. Once he rented the land of the old Grange Farm, from whence he transferred his modest horticultural products to a hollow, now covered by the houses in Circular Road, his residence in the midst of which was of the ship's cabin or discarded railway carriage type. He had formerly been in the service of Sir Piers Mostyn, at Talacre, a never-failing point of vantage with which he met every remonstrance. Ask him the name of a flower, and he at once, without a change of countenance replied with an apparently Latin appellation,* against which our ignorance was not proof, though we had our suspicions and determined to put his floral knowledge to the test. So we planted the crown of a pine-apple in a pot, and asked the authority what species of " cactus " it was? He was quite equal to the occasion, and immediately christened it in the dead language. But there was nothing that could by

* His acknowledgement for monies received was made in the form of a very ricketty cross.

any possibility be translated into " pine-apple," or anything else.

His brother Jimmy followed the same occupation. Some years previously he had been on his way to America in the capacity of man servant to a family from Birkenhead, on board the unfortunate " Ocean Monarch " when she took fire. The Prince de Joinville was passing in his yacht, and went to the rescue,* but poor Jimmy was never the same after; the shock had left him partly daft. One morning he started his occupation at so early an hour as to alarm his patrons by the sound of his scythe. When they discovered the cause of their inquietude they opened a window and asked if he would like to have a candle? He was slightly deformed, and when you met him, he had such a catching smile that no matter how bad a temper you were in, you must smile too. As Jimmy advanced in years he found his way to that refuge for destitute and worn out humanity—the Workhouse. There he was employed to sow potatoes. Then he thought he would see how things were going on in the world, and the workhouse portals closed against him. But on one dark night he was caught removing the apples of the earth which had grown to maturity. He was captured and presented at court. In reply as to what he had to say for himself, he said he had set the potatoes and thought he had the best right to them. The magistrate differed in opinion, and Jimmy went below to learn the difference between *meum* and *tuum*.

A Birkenhead working man, in comfortable circumstances, proposed to his wife that they should take a

---

* The Prince de Joinville afterwards made a sketch of the terrible scene, which realised a handsome sum on being raffled for the benefit of the sufferers.

trip to the Isle of Man. The good woman gladly fell in with his views, and donned her best attire. The steamboat had hardly started when she created the utmost confusion among the passengers by her signs of of distress and her petitions to be set ashore. Her excitement was caused by no marine fear, but she had become conscious that her prospective pleasure had blinded her to the fact that she had left home in her house-slippers.

In a house in Bridge street there dwelt a harmless old gentleman who daily took his stand at his gate minus his coat—as every lady approached he ran two or three rapid little steps towards her, and while a bright smile beamed upon his happy old face, he saluted her from his forehead, and then kissed his hand. Those who received this attention for the first time were startled, but the bulk of passers-by knew what to expect. One day he strayed away and was never heard of since. It is presumed he met with death.

Memory takes me back to the tradespeople, who were very worthy of note. Our local hairdresser was a most uncommon character; he was known as Mr. P., though his real name was Mr. B., but in undertaking the supervision of the coiffures of the ladies of Birkenhead he concealed his identity, as he imagined that his patronesses would object to be waited upon by a retired Music Hall artiste, which he was. Tell a tale, no man could match him. In the most barefaced manner he mimicked his customers, uttered the most audacious speeches, told the most arrant lies; but everybody forgave him, in fact encouraged him, and his last daring act afforded a fund of afternoon chat. He would tell you that he had been to Paris for the fashions, and the high society he had frequented, astounding his hearers with the nonchalant account he gave of having personally danced with the Empress at the Tuileries, and such like extravagances. One lady, more sceptical than the rest, questioned his long-suffering little wife as to the truth of his assertion. "Oh no, Ma'am; he was only looking in at the window, raised on someone's shoulders."

No one knew better than he how to trade on the foibles of the ladies; well was he aware that if Mrs. This bought a thing, Mrs. That would not be outdone. On his return from the Continent he would send a basket of Marie Louise pears (which he most likely purchased in the local market) to one of his customers, with the message that he had brought them from Paris, that Mrs. —— (her social competitor) had taken a similar basket, and the fruit were 6d. each. The messenger would be the bearer back of the cash value of the consignment, while the lady would afterwards discover that her rival friend had never even had any pears offered to her. His ready wit never deserted him, and he extricated himself either creditably or laughably (mostly the latter) out of every scrape. His personal appearance greatly resembled the waxen gentleman who revolved in his own shop window. His egregious vanity was such that he would don his best attire, survey himself in his *cheval* glass, and address himself as Lord P.

At this time there dwelt among us a music teacher, Mr. Henry Millar. The whole family of self, wife, sons and daughters, were a lovely choir in themselves. In spite of their recognised talents, they fared no better than most who trust to musical genius to support them, and Mr. Millar gave an annual concert to help

E

to make ends meet. As a matter of attraction, he secured the services of Mr. P., the hairdresser, who consented to sing "on this occasion only." The raid on tickets caused by this announcement secured their entire disposal. The concert took place in the Craven Rooms, Chester Street. The first appearance of Mr. P. was in character, "I'm a gent, I'm a gent, I'm a gent, ready made," to the air of "I'm afloat," his costume, the largest of checks, and the rest *en suite*. Before the conclusion of the entertainment he re-appeared and sang an impromptu, in which he imitated everybody who had taken part in the programme (himself included).

The *beneficiare* was so elated at the unusual success of his enterprise that he sent most of the audience into hysterics over his own performance of "God save the Queen." Never was so much energy displayed on that patriotic composition, he struck the chords on both ends of the instrument at the same time, and intermingled the most furious embellishments; in his excitement he gradually rose from his seat, and actually struck the finishing notes standing. When the company dispersed, they one and all said they had never enjoyed themselves so much in their lives. Poor old Millar, dead this many a day!

About the year 1850, not far from the ferry, there was a broker's shop, the shutters of which slid up and down. In the daytime they were supported by two old bedposts. The couple who owned it were keen, too keen, but respectable tradespeople. The woman was called one day to attend a customer who gave an immensity of trouble before she could make her purchase. After she left, a lady who was present, expressed sympathy that so little consideration had been shown, when she received the following ecstatic reply, " To the poorest of my customers who lays out but a penny in a pepper-box I feel so humble that I could lay down on the ground and let them wipe their feet upon me." *Reversi!* The modern tradesman would hardly feel abject for the purchase of a whole spice box !

The broker acted as plate-bearer to solicit the contributions of the faithful at his church ; a fellow-parishioner, a gentleman who frequently allowed his language to escape from control, gave him an extensive order in his branch of business. When the day of reckoning came, the account was far in excess of anticipation, and no remonstrance could produce an abatement. It was therefore paid. The next Sunday's service was on behalf of a charity, and as the plate was handed by victor to victim, it was pushed back with the accompaniment of these audible words, " No, you thief ! "

One afternoon the female element of this institution ran after me to enquire after my mother's health. Hearing that it was satisfactory, she delivered herself of this rigmarole of cant, " Render acceptable to your mama my most grateful tribute of homage and respect, and tell her that I would any day sooner see her smile than her money." How far her servility was genuine may be gathered from the following episode. I had been sent with a younger sister to settle a rather large account, and asked these two arch-hypocrites to allow discount, which they refused, although they had taken *carte blanche* in the execution of the order. However, the old man, who was just a shade more sincere than his wife, slipped a two-shilling piece into my sister's hand ; the mean old woman intercepted her before she reached the door, and took the coin from her. That was the last transaction between us.

Our butcher was a most worthy man, and his wife even surpassed him in excellence. She always reminded me of Dickens' apple-faced woman, with her pretty, rosy cheeks, and plump, good-tempered face. We were on the best of terms, and always had a gossip. One day she was telling of the satisfactory education her boys were receiving in Yorkshire, where the fee was only £20 per annum, but there were no holidays, no carpets on the bedroom floors, and the lads had to wear thick boots (clogs, if I remember rightly). I took my mother unawares by chiming in, " They must be at Mr. Squeers." *   " No," said the motherly butcheress, " I don't think that is the name." This good couple may be numbered among the lucky few who realised a fortune in Birkenhead, for a prosperous career enabled them to spend their latter days in their own hall.

Almost opposite to this worthy couple there dwelt a tailor. Like any other tradesman he was sometimes left regretting the absence of some of his patrons, who would sail for foreign climes without going through the formality of wishing him farewell; indeed, by this oversight on their part, he fared badly. To revenge himself for these slights, he would paste upon his shop windows such notices as, " Mr. —— owes me ——; d——d scamp, gone to Canada," or elsewhere, as the case might be. Gentlemen, *en route* for the ferry, invariably crossed the road in a morning to inspect the latest additions. May be he was aggravated. There is no retort without attack—his customers dwelt

* Dickens' Yorkshire Schoolmaster, whose terms and conditions were much the same.

in Oxton, and Oxton was called "Swindle Hill."
Upon one occasion he was entrusted with the repairs
of the canonicals of the late Canon Chapman; he
donned the garments himself, and hied away to an
artist's studio, where he obtained a copy of his act of
sacrilege.

CHAPTER IX.

Old Betty Griffiths — George Lance's Little Joke — The Gallant Colonel — The Horse bears the Major away — The first Street-Railway — The Explosion of the " Lottie Sleigh."

The first lady's nurse in Birkenhead was Betty Griffiths, an active old body. herself a grandmother. She wore a short petticoat of red and black stripes, and large check apron, with two pockets, one of which held her ball of wool, for knitting was her constant occupation. Her head-covering on week days was a " Jim Crow " hat, on Sundays the high Welsh hat. Children always addressed her as " Mother Griffiths," for she claimed almost every child as her own. So respected was she when she died, that the ladies whom she had attended, sent black to drape the mortuary room, a custom then prevalent, the material afterwards being converted into mourning dresses for the relatives. The ladies themselves followed old Betty Griffiths to her grave in St. Mary's churchyard. Hearses were not in vogue among the poorer class, and a corpse would be carried to its resting place by six friends, who would volunteer to do this last kindness.

Flaybrick Hill was meanwhile being converted into a place of interment for the rising generation who now so thickly occupy it. By a strange coincidence, the first to be interred therein was he who laid the foundation stone, Mr. Philip Morton.

There lies at rest, in Flaybrick Hill Cemetery, our great English fruit and still life painter, George Lance. His simple headstone merely records his name and date of death, with the emblems of his craft, the brushes and palette. He was one morning walking down Victoria Road, New Brighton, with his son-in-law, Mr. Bower, when the spirit of fun moved him to play a part in the following incident: Halfway up the road there used to stand the hut-like shop of an old man named Peat; by title "the father of the place." For did not our fathers and grandfathers tell us that they had had *their* buckets and spades purchased at his modest repository for seaside wares. Everybody knew him, and what was more important, he knew everybody, and at all hours he stationed himself at his door to tackle the unwary, and pin them with a gossip. He had attempted the artistic, and whitewashed the outside of his house, and smeared it with things that always provoked the query "What are these?" "Trees" he would proudly answer, and lead off with the previously alluded-to tale. "One morning," he would say, "Mr. Lance and Mr. Bower were walking down to the boat, when Mr. Lance drew his companion's attention to the trees. "They are only painted," said Mr. Bower. "No, they are real," said the artist. Then the old man would add, triumphantly, "it was only when he came and touched them that he was convinced they were painted." No living creature could honestly have traced any affinity between the old man's production and nature, and Lance's error was the result of the designer being within earshot.

Who is this? " the gallant Colonel," and why?
for set him astride a horse, and there at once you had
a test of his courage. As it was consistent with his
position in the Volunteer Corps that he should give
the word of command " *à Cheval*," a tame, white old
circus horse was purchased, whereon he might sit in
assumed confidence. In a morning he would mount
at his door, assisted by his groom, who would then
walk to the ferry, to take charge of the animal on the
return home. Invariably the man arrived at the goal
before his master, who would ride leisurely along,
calmly surveying the country, as if it were his will to
go slowly—which it decidedly was.

At a review in the Park, the band unknowingly
played an air familiar to the broken down brute. Old
memories were revived, and its ancient legs performed
an ungraceful waltz, whilst its rider clung to its mane
in terror. The groom, who always stood at hand to
avert a catastrophe, arrested the mazy movement, and
word was sent to the musicians to change the tune.

Equine pranks have more than once upset the
dignity of a review. In the Upper Park, a popular
Major was issuing orders to his corps of volunteers
(the 1st Cheshire) which sounded like " Oof, oof, er."
But it must have meant something, for the rifles
quickly passed from right to left, while " Er, er, oof,"
sent the weapons back. One special injunction was
uttered in such stentorian tones that the horse upon
which the Major was seated took fright, and galloped
away as if all the foul fiends were in pursuit, right
across the field, where there was not a living soul.
The noble Major had his men well under command,
but was himself subservient to brute power, and away
he was carried, while the multitude laughed heartily,

and the battalion remained motionless awaiting their commander's return. How slowly and humbly he rode back.

Birkenhead may claim the honour of having been selected by Mr. G. F. Train as a land of promise wherein to lay down the first street railways in Europe. The opening took place on August 30, 1860. A procession of flag-bedecked cars traversed the streets, Mr. Train himself leading on the first. At the banquet given at night to commemorate the event, he intimated that he had invited all the crowned heads in Europe, including his Holiness the Pope, to be present. As none of the exalted powers accepted, nor did he read any reasons for august absence, we may assume that the statement was merely one of those extensions of probabilities peculiarly American.

The original lines were not sunk level with the ground, but were somewhat raised, and where they intersected each other, the jolt in any vehicle not specially prepared, was fearful. The cabmen had a rare spite against the novelties, and rejoiced in taking their fares over the road containing most crossings of rails. As they approached them, the drivers would whip up their steeds, and attack the lines with a rush that sent the occupants flying up off their seats, and down with a bump; all done to set people against the innovations. It was no unusual thing to find a car with its passengers on terra firma, while appliances were used to replace the vehicle on the rails. Then the cabmen commenced a system of persecution, and you would meet a car crawling along at tortoise pace behind an obstructive cab that blocked its progress. Every useful invention has had to contend against similar difficulties, and found itself retarded by the impediment of prejudice. The inventor has often run his course before its value is recognised, and then we wonder how we did without things that have passed through heart-breaking struggles to assert themselves.

About 6 o'clock on the evening of January 15, 1864, our very foundations were shaken by a violent explosion. A vessel laden with gunpowder, named the *Lottie Sleigh* lay in the Sloyne. The mate, in trimming a paraffin lamp, upset it, and the blazing oil ran upon the deck. Knowing the perilous cargo that was stored below, he signalled for assistance, which speedily arrived in the old Rock Ferry boat *Wasp*, captain Joe Hughes,* that ran alongside, and took off the crew of the doomed ship. They had hardly withdrawn to a safe distance when a terrific explosion ensued. The passengers on board the relieving steamer said the shock was so great that they seemed to jump a yard out of the water. We lived a mile and a quarter from the scene of the disaster, and when it happened, I was playing chess with a sister, we left the game for a time, and on resuming it, we found that the concussion had caused every man on the board to move an inch from his place. The whole of the town verging on the river was wrecked completely. On the following Sunday there was to be seen a sight without parallel in our annals. Hamilton Square, said to be one of the finest squares in England, had almost every pane of glass broken by the disaster, and day of rest as it should have been, every

---

* After spending the greater part of his life as captain of this steamer, to which Mr. Hughes was so attached for her pliable qualities that he used to say she would do everything but speak, he applied for assistance from the parish at the age of 73, and was offered " the house "--a degradation averted by the kindness of friends.

house had glaziers at work repairing the damages. All the glass in the vicinity was exhausted, and a raid for supply made on St. Helens. Hence the necessity of working on Sunday.

As the approaches to the ferry deteriorated, the owner of two good houses near the river, alive to the disadvantage of their position, removed them to surroundings befitting their style which would prove more remunerative. The stones were dissected and re-erected in Park Road South, where they now stand numbered 90 and 92.

CHAPTER X.

MUSICAL RECOLLECTIONS—MESDAMES GRISI, ALBONI,
GUARABELLA GASSIER, AND JENNY LIND — THE
GERMAN HERR SPECULATES IN PRODIGIES.

THE Music Hall, in Claughton Road, was erected by
the Liverpool Philharmonic Society, assisted by private subscription. When I look at the Hall I think
of its departed glory. How few of the present day
people know of the matchless voices that have
echoed within it walls. Grisi the incomparable;
Alboni her companion in opera, whose massive figure
caused her illustrious master, Rossini, to say, jocularly,
that she was an elephant who had swallowed a
nightingale; Mme. Guarabella with her romantic history of marriage to a Russian Court official, who
endeavoured to repudiate it on the grounds that he
had not received the requisite permission of the Czar;
the wife's representation to the Autocrat of Russia,
who sent for the couple and acknowledged the union.
The lady made one obeisance to the Czar, and another
to her husband, and left him for ever to achieve fame
on the operatic stage.

There also sang Mme. Gassier, whose flexible voice
as a Spanish servant attracted the notice of a music
master in search of a novelty, who developed its bril-
liant execution. How few recollect her rendering in
that hall of the florid vocal waltz specially composed

for her by Venzano "*Ah che assorta*," introducing a prolonged shake as the waltz proceeds.

Mdlle. Thérése Titjens, too, sang in one of the series of Concerts. A large lively woman, full of good humour, on whom the mantle of Grisi was said to have descended. The following anecdote will give an idea of her sense of fun. I was one of those selected in London to assist the local choirs at one of the Worcester festivals. The lady principals were Mdlle. Titjens, Mme. Lemmens Sherrington, and Mme. Patey. In the ladies' room, Mme. Lemmens Sherrington retired unassumingly in a corner, smiling quietly at all that was going on. Mme. Patey, clad in lemon satin, sat stately and erect, while her maid stood beside her, and with outstretched hands protected any unwary encroachment on the dress. Would her mistress have moved to avert a calamity? Oh no, decidedly not.

Mdlle. Titjens was all life and chatter. When preparing to depart, *her* maid said, " Madame, your dress is on the floor." " Oh," said the unaffected songstress "I don't mind the silk skirt, but I do want to save this " (a white grenadine upper skirt). Saying which, she raised it, and threw it over her head, where its stiffness caused it to assume the form used by bad intentioned persons who cover themselves with their garment to terrify children. She glanced at herself in the glass, and then bent down to me as I sat by the dressing table. " Now," whispered she, in broken English, " if a ghost shall see me he will be frightened of me."

Shortly after Grisi sang in Birkenhead, she appeared in farewell opera in Liverpool. I had the privilege of hearing her in " Norma," which was con-

sidered her grandest exposition, and she stands out in
my memory as no opera singer since heard could
imprint herself. Her stately massive figure so suitable
to represent the Druidical priestess, entered down an
incline, and with her sickle cut the mistletoe, sacred
emblem of her faith, and distributed it to her sister-
hood. As the moon slowly rose, she advanced to the
front, extended her arms upwards, and sang the
invocation to the Goddess whom they worshipped in
that luminary " Casta Diva." The last scene, in which
she is about to be sacrificed on the burning pyre, could
never be effaced from the remembrance of anyone
who had witnessed it. The stage, covered with
figures, the Druids endeavouring to bind her with
black linen, her efforts at resistance, with struggling,
bare, uplifted arms; as band, principals, and chorus
reached the summit of their power, the one grand
voice surpassed them all, conveying a thrill of awe
by its supreme volume.

For a few seasons, very enjoyable ballad concerts
were given in the Drill Hall, near Monk's Ferry. The
artistes were mostly of local fame, and foremost among
the favourites were Mr. and Mrs. Scarisbrick and their
pupils, Edith and Kate Wynne, and Mr. W. Ryalls,
principals of the choir of St. Peter's Roman Catholic
Chapel, Seel Street, Liverpool, where Sims Reeves
sang during the six months that he fulfilled an engagement at the old Liver Theatre in Church Street.
Mrs. Scarisbrick was unusually massive in appearance,
with a very kind face. She invariably paid double fare
in an omnibus. Once she entered one of these public
conveyances while it was stationary. Presently a
woman came up to the door, and looked anxiously
along the seats on either side, then she exclaimed,

" Oh lady, lady, you have sat upon my bird." " True enough," said Mrs. Scarisbrick, who used to tell the tale against herself, " it never lived to tell the tale, it was in a little wicker cage, and I had crushed it quite flat." At the above named popular Concerts, the costume of the younger ladies who sang, would be composed of book muslin over some cheap material, such as glazed calico, and their roses had bloomed for many a day, and bore testimony to their prolonged blooming. A year or two's finishing touches in London, placed Edith Wynne at the head of our ballad singers ; her attire became satin and point lace, and her earnings £2,000 a year.

As this is a chapter of musical reminiscences, interesting mention may be made of that Queen of Song, Jenny Lind, whose capricious temper made her a strange contradiction of a woman—sometimes so disagreeable, sometimes so affable. The succeeding anecdotes will exemplify her capabilities in this regard. Somewhere in the eighteen-forties she had an engagement in Liverpool, during which she was the guest of a fellow-country woman. This lady, thinking to give pleasure to the great singer, invited a few of her select coterie to spend the evening at her house. When Jenny Lind heard of this intended kindness, she declared she would not go into the room, and was very angry, and according to English ideas, very rude. However, she was coaxed into going down stairs on the condition that she should not see anybody, and that she might sit concealed behind the folding doors of the drawing room. The dismay and uncomfortable position of the hostess and her friends can well be imagined. Presently a gentleman (since dead) sang that song of songs " Adelaida." The charming voice and exquisite pathos had its effect on more than one hearer. Jenny Lind's head was seen to crane forward from behind the folding doors. When he had finished she emerged from her seclusion, advanced to the singer, and made herself most agreeable. During the same visit, she one day passed through the library where her host's sons were at lessons with their tutor, a delicate looking, poor, young man, who when he saw her, stood up with an expression on his face as of a devotee worshipping at the shrine of his celestial saint. Something in his attitude struck Jenny Lind, and created a feeling of curiosity regarding him. She asked who he was? and when told how he craved to hear her sing, but had not the means to pay for a ticket of admission to the Concert that night, she laughingly said "*Pauvre diable*, I'll sing to him," and proceeding to the piano she ravished the ears of the humble listener with song after song from her choice *repertoire*. The last time when this singer beyond compare was heard in Liverpool was for the benefit of the Southern Hospital, when, if I remember rightly, she generously gave her services gratuitously on behalf of the charity. The price of tickets was as high as a guinea each. She afterwards paid a visit to the institution, during which she was presented with a beautiful bracelet as an acknowledgement of her Christian charity on behalf of suffering humanity. When she saw it she exclaimed, " Oh, you know, I did not wish this," and she burst into tears. We must remember her at her best, for she was a good woman.

Once upon a time there dwelt in Liverpool a professor of music who kept his weather eye open in search of a prodigy wherewith to speculate. The first he discovered was in company of a street organ, outpouring its untrained sweetness to an encircling crowd. The youth who had attracted him by his vocal gift was easily induced to better his condition and accept the offer of the musician that he should place himself in his hands, to perfect his beautiful voice under instruction, for which the master was to be repaid by—payment by results. In due course the prodigy made his *rentrée* in public under more favourable aspects than when he made his first appearance. The professor had fed, clothed, and bought him a breastpin. The new-comer filled a vacuum that had long been empty in the world of song, and the musical publications re-echoed his successes. But—how did he repay his teacher? He left him. If there had been an agreement, it only tended to demonstrate that law is not justice, for the Courts declared against it, while the German Herr shook his head, and thought it an ungrateful world—very.*

The next speculation he ventured upon was a talented young lady with a beautiful voice. He and this pupil appeared together at many high class concerts. He applied to the organist of one of the principal Roman Catholic Churches in Liverpool, soliciting that Miss—— and himself might sing the offertory piece on some occasion. Knowing their superior qualifications the request was acceded to, and the next Sunday morning's service appointed for the display. As the organist drove down in his hansom, he saw the " Herr " walking outside the sacred edifice, and waived his hand to him. Presently from his vantage ground of observation he noticed the young lady's mother piloted in state up the aisle, and deposited in one of the front pews. The service com-

---

* At the trial, the professor regretted the gift of the breastpin.

F

menced, but the lady and gentleman had not entered the choir. As they were only to sing after the sermon, it was assumed that they would arrive before its conclusion, but it ended, and they came not. The organist now began to feel awkward, as he had not anticipated a *fiasco*. So he started an impromptu, thinking the absentees might still appear. From his elevated post he saw the lady mother below, turn and turn again in the direction of the choir, in evident wonder at the vocal silence. But the impromptu meandered on alone, to the sole accompaniment of the clatter of the coin on the collecting plates. When the faithful had deposited their offerings the service was resumed by the resident choir.

It afterwards transpired that the professor, learning wisdom by experience had determined to legally secure his prize with its possible profits, and induced the young lady to link her fate with his. The engagement to sing was merely a ruse to entrap the elder lady into enforced detention while the two delinquents eloped. Marry in haste and repent at leisure! Before many years had passed the bride had proved the truth of the adage, and sought judicial severance of the knot that had been so craftily tied. This was effected on very good grounds; after which she ran up the histrionic ladder with great rapidity, and remained in that elevated position as a leading lady in her profession—comic opera.

CHAPTER XI.

The Romantic Career of the Beautiful Miss O.—
Jane Clarke, the Milliner—The Manchester
Mummy—Mr. B., M.P., accepts the Cheque—
"The Wasp" stings the Editor.

The next story I propose to narrate is what may
correctly be called a "romance" that was quietly
enacted in our midst, and though some will remember
the principal actress, they lost sight of her when she
soared to higher regions, therefore I feel sure they will
welcome an account of her wonderful career.

Many years ago their lived in Hamilton Square an
exceedingly kind hearted lady. She could lay claim
to certain pardonable peculiarities, and no small
fortune was expended on personal adornment, which
was of the best and loudest quality; her cameo
brooch contained a whole Roman war, and her gold
chain would have held a small vessel at anchor. She
would tell you that her mother was a " Porrtugee "
lady, and we thought how very much akin was
" Porrtugee " English, as spoken by that lady, to the
lingo of Cambria's daughters ; her partialities were all
in favour of Wales and its people, while her brother
bore a true Welsh surname ; but she was a good
motherly soul. She engaged a lady as daily governess
to her children, and noticing that she possessed a very
fine voice, she offered the use of her piano to her
young teacher, whom we will call Miss O. Thinking

the talent was worthy of culture, the worthy woman
wrote to Jenny Lind (Mme. Goldschimdt) and asked
her advice. In reply, she received the notification
from the great singer that she would be in Birming-
ham on a certain day, and if Mrs. W. liked to bring her
protégée she would hear her sing and pass her opinion.
The governess was of exceedingly good family, mentioned in Ormerod's history of Cheshire ; her father
had migrated to the West Indies, and there, owing to
his being guarantee for a defaulting friend, his fortune
was swamped, his health broken, and he died, leaving
his widow and really beautiful daughters penniless.
Mrs. W. generously defrayed all expenses to Birming-
ham ; the verdict was favourable, and so spake the
Queen of Song, " Her vocal training will be expensive,
there might be friends who would subscribe the cost,
and if that can be managed, write me word by what
train the young lady will arrive in London, and my
carriage shall meet her at the station."   The husband
of Mrs. W. was a man of influence, and in a short
time he raised a few hundred pounds from old friends
of the young lady's father in Manchester and Liverpool, and the services of the governess were dispensed
with to enable her to better her prospects.   The funds
were deposited with a gentleman of standing, and
Madame's carriage met the appointed train, and conveyed the aspirant to her house, where she remained
her guest for a considerable time.   Her personal
appearance was strikingly lady-like, manners and
deportment refined, stately, and fascinating.   Her
studies were commenced under Balfe and Garcia.

Balfe was then composing his opera " Satanella,"
Miss Louisa Pyne to take the title *rôle*.   She bore so
great a resemblance to her Majesty Queen Victoria

that the part of a queen was constantly introduced
into operas in which Miss Pyne would sing, such as
the " Rose of Castile," and when she advanced up
the stage in regal attire, the similarity was striking,
and always evoked loud applause.

Despite the great extension of favour shown by
Jenny Lind, her variable temper marred the pleasure
of constant association. At seven in the morning she
would sit chatting on her visitor's bed, and at breakfast time she would be unbearable.

At the expiration of six months the gentleman who
held the money in trust failed in business, and in the
catastrophe the money subscribed disappeared. In
order to continue her lessons, Miss O. took a situation
in a ladies' school on the outskirts of London, and the
salary she earned enabled her to resume vocal instruction, but her limited means prohibited expenditure,
and the journey to and from London was made many
a day without breaking her fast; this deprivation
threw her into a bad state of health, and the doctor
who attended the school was consulted; he guessed
the real cause of her ailment, and considerately told
her to call and see his wife, which she did, with the
result that she was always detained to luncheon. The
two ladies became so much attached to each other
that the doctor's wife induced her new friend to resign
her position in the school and reside with her, the pair
living in sisterly harmony until a sensible maiden aunt
advised Miss O. that she ought to make use of her
talents on her own behalf, and not burden friends, to
which end she returned to her mother's house in
Birkenhead, in the locality of Bridge Street. I have
known the good " Porrtugee " lady don a large cloak
on a Saturday night and personally leave Sunday's

requirements *incog.* for the use of the widow lady.
About this time I became a pupil, and continue the
story from actual knowledge. She was asked to sing
at the Liverpool Philharmonic Hall. Her staunch
friend and former mistress took her to Jane Clarke's
world renowned emporium to select the dress to be
worn on the auspicious occasion, and with her good
natured lavishness she promised to contribute ten
pounds towards the cost. The costume provided was
lemon-coloured moiré, trimmed with swansdown, so
suitable to her perfectly oval face and olive com-
plexion; her head, surmounted by massive coils of
black hair, was decorated with cut steel stars, worn
coronet-wise. The vocal demonstration, however, was
a thorough *fiasco*, as thorough as was ever witnessed
within those select walls! Her first song was Balfe's
charming ballad " The green trees whispered," and
many bars were not passed before a flood of memory
rushed before the singer; the remembrance of the days
when she was one of a County family in honoured position, and her changed fortune, standing on a public plat-
form, singing to support her mother; for in those days
ladies did *not* court notoriety on the boards. The tears
welled up to her eyes, her voice quavered, then there
was an utter break-down, and she was forced to retire;
a few moments were given to allow her to recover herself, but on her re-appearance the same thing happened, and she was led off. Her second song was
omitted from the programme; yet, strange to say, next
morning's papers contained only graceful expressions
of sympathy, and what is so unusual in making reference to the fair vocalists at the Philharmonic Hall,
they dilated on her stately presence, to use their own
words " her graceful *personnel*." Her beauty had won all

hearts! One more public appearance she made, and only one, at the " Argyle Rooms," Birkenhead, our then fashionable concert hall. Here she contrived to offend her audience though she successfully executed her part in the programme. Seated in the front row were the family of one of our local magnates, who, with unpardonable bad breeding, levelled their opera glasses full in her face; she recognised the gentleman as having been her father's hatter in the days when a well made hat in Liverpool was familiarly known as a L—. The look of indignant scorn which she cast upon her annoyer was taken to themselves by the audience at large. From that day forth she aban: doned Concert singing as a bad business—a very bad business.

In due time she received the bill for the becoming lemon moiré dress; the amount, £20, stunned her; where could she find the £10 which fell to her to pro· vide? She went with her trouble to the good friend who had introduced her to Jane Clarke; the truly generous woman defrayed the whole cost, and released her from anxiety. Ah me! that fortune should fade from such liberal hands. I am sorry to say that it did. When I stand by the grave of this most kind-hearted woman in the cemetery, the whole of this tale passes in review before me. " The good men do lives after them."

One morning Miss O. received two letters from the Countess of S. and Earl D., to the effect that if she went up to London they might make it worth her while to do so. She begged to be excused from a week's tuition, and on her return home she laid before her very limited number of pupils (three, I think,) the proposition that had been made, and which she wished

gratefully to accept. The Earl alluded to was a
known musical patron and sincere friend to persons
of talent whose limited means prevented the perfecting
of their natural gifts. Out of his ample wealth he had
offered to defray the expenses of finishing touches
from master hands, and she departed to avail herself
of his generosity, Her lessons commenced under
Vera and Benedict. When about twelve months had
elapsed, she received the intelligence that her mother
was dangerously ill, in fact, dying. Her small means
forbade the expense of a railway journey, and she was
so overcome with grief as to be unable to take her
lesson. During the day the Earl called upon her, and
said, "Mr. Benedict tells me you did not attend this
morning, how was that?" She informed him of her
mother's serious illness, to which he made response,
"Then if she is so ill, why are you not with her? Are
you not friendly?" "Oh yes, my lord," she replied,
"but *you* could never understand the reason." "Oh,
I see, I see," he said, and getting out his cheque book,
he filled in the amount for twenty pounds, which he
handed to her saying, "Now, go and see your mother."
She hurried homeward, but the poor lady died while
her daughter was in the train; still she had the gratifi-
cation of hearing of her dear mother's last hours. At
the expiration of eighteen months she returned to
Birkenhead; her small income necessitated a humble
dwelling, and she took two rooms over a stationer's
shop, kept by a widow lady in Oxton Road. I have
seen her dining off the humblest of fare, which she
would laugh over, yet the dress on her back was made
by the Princess of Wales's dressmaker. Her costumes
were ever the essence of simplicity and elegance.
Gossip said that Bold Street firms supplied her with

bonnets, and made her sister's garments gratis, as advertisements. I never ascertained that to be an actual fact, and from my knowledge of her haughty character, have my own doubts of its accuracy.

Her grandfather had given a young soldier, afterwards a distinguished general, his outfit and a ten pound note when he started in life, and her grandmother bought his commission—there was some relationship between them. One day I asked her if he made any return to her for the assistance received from her relatives in the early portion of his career. She said, " Sometimes he asked me to breakfast with him, and once he gave me a cheque, but I returned it without looking at the amount." The reason for non-acceptance lay in the fact that it might have been tendered much earlier. Some of her pupils made her humble offerings of cheese-cakes and fresh eggs, which were always accepted with the good fellowship intended. As she extended her acquaintance in Birkenhead, she naturally received invitations to join its festivities. In her costume of plain white muslin, and necklace of large imitation pearls, with her massive hair plaited as a coronet, she moved like an empress. Her pupils at no time exceeded eight, indeed, rarely reached that number. Poor as she unquestionably was at that time, she was exceedingly independent, and would never apply for a prospective pupil, saying, " They know where I am to be found, and if they want me they can call upon me."

Occasionally presents arrived bearing an Earl's coronet, mostly of a useless description to her, such as wine that she did not drink, and game and hares that she could not cook.

As in London, so in Birkenhead, she charmed

such as she liked, and latterly gave up her lowly
rooms to pass by invitation from one house to
another. She casually met an old lady with whom
she had prior acquaintance in more fortunate days.
On this lady's return to her home in Chester, she sent
a letter to Miss O, and these are the real and true
words of the missive: " My dear, you are too good for
Birkenhead; come here (on such a day) and I will ask
some of the Cathedral people to meet you, and see
what can be done for you." The invitation was
accepted. The Dean of that day told her he re-
membered her as a little girl, and her all round
welcome was so warm that, from within a week
that day, Birkenhead knew her no more. Chester
provided numerous pupils, among whom were the
daughters of the veteran Lord C., who drove in sixteen
miles, and invariably took a well-packed hamper for
her acceptance. After two years' residence in Chester
she obtained an enviable appointment in a notoriously
wealthy London family; her duties were to sit in the
room while the young ladies took their lessons, ride
with them in the Park, and accompany them to the
Opera. After which she was successively reader to a
millionaire baroness, and lady housekeeper to a titled
bachelor medical gentleman. From thence she was
transferred as companion to the Dowager Countess of
D., who, on her deathbed, gave her a ring valued at
£400, and bequeathed her as a legacy to a rich cousin
aged eighty. When this old gentleman died he left
her the handsome sum of £60,000. Thus everything
rights itself in the end. Few histories are so full of
social adventure. Her eldest sister made a good
match in Liverpool, and totally ignored her from the
day on which she started to earn her own living.

Eventually the heroine of this story married a Major in the army.

The "Jane Clarke" to whom reference was made in the preceding tale, was a noted Liverpool milliner. She had earned her world-renowned reputation by the elegant lady-like bonnets she produced. No one could lay a flower as she laid it. She was personally a dark swarthy woman, plain in looks. In a morning she would appear in a point lace dressing-gown, each finger and even her thumbs bejewelled with gems that she called "the Clarke jewels." The show-room was full of most valuable works of art taken from customers to wipe off bad debts. She presented the beautiful picture, "The Blind Beggar," to the National Gallery.

She had most peculiar ideas, and did not believe in death! She left instructions that she was to be bathed and pinched for a certain number of days after her collapse, and if she did not resume consciousness after this course of treatment, she might be interred. She *is* interred! She had great faith in pinching, and when afflicted by any ailment one of her young ladies would have to exercise upon the aching spot. To combat toothache she would say "pinch your gum, and do not tell your dentist I told you to do so." Meaning that it would prove an infallible remedy which would deprive the dentist of his fee, or in other words, "make one pain to cure another."

Somewhat similar in the horror of being buried alive, was an old lady near Manchester. She willed a large sum of money to her relatives which they were to enjoy so long as she remained unburied. If at any time she was put under ground, the money was to lapse to certain charities. When she died, her body was embalmed and placed in an upright case in a corner of one of the rooms in the Peter Street Museum, Manchester. After some time the authorities decided to bury her. Then came a contest over the cash ; she was unearthed and replaced in her old show case, while her stone coffin in which an endeavour had been made to evade the legal difficulty, found its way to a field as a drinking trough for horses. Her face looked as if covered with pitch, but the features were perfect, even to such details as the eyelashes. The whole appearance was just like a marine store dealer's black doll.

When children are young they mostly have a horrid brother, and we were no better off in that respect than any other family. One day the spirit of mischief moved him to bring a frog and place it in our midst on the dining room floor. We had the most intense dislike to these creatures of uncertain movement, and grouped ourselves ignominiously in a corner, as far from its gyrations as possible. Our father was habitually very reserved among us, but out of sheer pity he took the fire shovel, and assumed the most grotesque attitudes for a usually stately man, while he tried to coax the frog to take a seat upon the shovel. In this he was at last successful, and proceeded with steady hand to carry his prize from the room. Suddenly he gave a most involuntary start, and let the shovel drop, the frog had shown a preferable tendency to take a seat on him.

When this youth grew up he did not mend his ways, he spared neither friend nor stranger if he saw in him the substance for a practical joke. Arrangements with the London press caused his removal to the Metropolis. Not long after he entered upon these

engagements, the late Mr. B., M.P., had become
entangled with an elderly maiden lady living in Paris,
and he had committed such indiscretions and follies,
(for a man well on in years,) as kissing her foot when
he put on her boot. This she considered sufficient
groundwork for an action for breach of promise, in
which the defendant was mulcted in £300 damages.
He then received a letter from the young artist, expressive of sympathy, stating that he considered the
verdict against evidence, and as he was wishful to
convey some appreciation of his (the M.P.'s) efforts
on behalf of Ireland (between ourselves he had no
interest whatever in the Green Isle), he begged his
acceptance of the accompanying cheque for £400
towards expenses.

The recipient replied that he did not know what he
had done to merit such kindness, but concluded by
accepting it. After posting his thanks he adjourned
to the bank to cash the cheque. It was handed back
to him with the words endorsed upon it, " No effects,"
after which, he thought the less he said about that
matter the better.

The record of circumstances attending the birth of
The Wasp, (a satirical local paper conducted some few
years ago by the aforenamed artist) may be found
amusing. The young editor issued 800 copies of
No. 1, and sent them round to the various bookstalls.
After a day or two he made a tour of inspection, and,
seeing none of the numbers on the stalls, he concluded
they were all sold, and forthwith printed 1,000 copies
of No. 2. One evening he returned home leaving his
elder brother (who was temporarily one of his staff)
to close the *office*. While occupying this position they
always addressed each other as " Sir," in mock

courtesy, and when the subordinate joined the family circle, the following conversation ensued between the brothers:—

Sub. " Bad news, sir."

Editor. " What is it, sir, out with it ? "

Sub. " Paper returned, sir."

Editor. How many copies, sir ? "

Sub. " Guess, sir."

Editor. " A dozen."

Sub. " No, sir, guess again."

Editor. " Well, two dozen ? Be brief sir, how many ? "

Sub. " They have every one been returned unopened, sir, not one parcel has been undone."

If the 1,000 copies of No 2 had not been printed, most probably they never would have been ; but out they went and took root, and the satirical little journal eventually brought in a good remuneration to its proprietor.

One more sketch of by-gone days before closing this chapter. A gay old lady kept hospitable house, and modestly entertained her extensive circle of acquaintance in an evening. Most pleasant people met in her drawing-room, and all would go well until a song from the hostess was announced, without which no assembly was ever allowed to close. How every guest dreaded the moment of display, and sat with braced nerves, avoiding each other's eyes, as the feeble old voice piped forth, " She wore a wreath of roses." But more unbearable still was her rendering of—

> Thou, thou reign'st in this bo-o-o-som,
> There, there hast thou thy thro-o-one,
> Am I not fondly thine own?

The prolonged *roulade* which preceded the final word, and the intense look of love which she cast upon her admiring old spouse, who always led the applause, were too much for the audience, and one of the best behaved ladies in the world used to say that, whenever she knew that this song had been asked for, she endeavoured to quit the room, and if that could not be done, she turned over the leaves of the music for the singer, with her back to the company. Though the voice of the songstress has been silent for many a year, its recollection still brings a hearty laugh from the false friends who applauded.

THE PROMENADE AND PAYGATES AT WOODSIDE FERRY IN 1850.

CHAPTER XII.

THE GREAT WIRRAL FOREST—KING WILLIAM THE
THIRD IN CHESHIRE—LEASOWE CASTLE—LADY C.
DISAPPOINTS THE VOLUNTEERS—THE MAGISTRATES
DISAPPEAR FROM IMAGINARY FOES.

IN ancient times it is asserted that the Great Wirral
Forest extended from Chester to the Irish Sea. Evidence exists of the remains of giant trees submerged
in the sea between Leasowe and Hoylake, while the
name of our own ferry, " Woodside," bespeaks that
the face of nature is changed. In the blue clay which
covers the submarine forest, the horns of the red deer,
and also the skulls and horns of two species of wild
oxen have been found. In 1864 a human skeleton was
discovered, the bones of which were encrusted with
marine creatures, barnacles, etc. It was presented to
the Museum of the Royal College of Surgeons in London, as being probably the remains of a pre-historic
man, that is of an inhabitant of the district in times
long anterior to the Roman invasion.

At very low tides traces of tombstones have been
found. In 1828 a number of skeletons were disinterred
below low water mark, their regularity and position
are evidence that a church once stood on that point
called Lees Kirk, but the element which respected not
Canute demolished the edifice. The Kirk may serve
as a solution to the mystic utterance of the famous
Cheshire prophet Nixon, as he sat on the brow of

Storeton Hill, brooding over the wickedness of his fellow men. When questioned by his friend, the miller, as to where a man should take refuge on the day of coming evil, the seer replied, " In God's croft, between the Mersey and the Dee." He may have alluded to the hallowed sanctuary of the sacred edifice now submerged at that point.

An ancient rhyme records—

> From Birkethead untill Hilbree
> A squirrel can hop from tree to tree.

The scene is so changed that if the squirrel wishes to take his return journey, he must do it on *terra firma*, the few gnarled trunks alone remain to show where the forest once flourished, and these, too, are rapidly being washed away.

Hearing to seek and find was peculiarly applicable to relics of Saxon presence at this spot, I have burrowed by the hour, and never found anything but an old shaving brush, which I discarded as a luxury unknown to the early Saxons. After my bootless search, I came to the conclusion that our antecedents were not so careless of their money and jewellery as they have been accredited.

In June, 1690, King William the Third tarried nigh this locality *en route* for Ireland, and the battle of the Boyne. On the 9th of that month he slept at Peel Hall, near Tarvin, the seat of Colonel Roger Whiteley. The next day being Sunday, he attended service at Chester Cathedral, and, the same afternoon, proceeded to Gayton Hall, near Parkgate, the residence of William Glegg, Esq., where Sir Cloudesley Shovel and other commanders awaited his arrival. He remained the night. Before his departure next morning, he knighted his host, and granted to him and his heirs for ever, the free fishery of the Dee, which right is now exercised by his descendants.

His Majesty quitted Gayton for Leasowe, where the troops were encamped.* On his arrival, tents were struck, and all embarked from the point of Hoyle Lake, now called " King's Gap " to commemorate the event. Mr. Edward Tarlton, of the ship *James*, of Liverpool, acted as pilot upon the occasion, and conducted His Majesty on to a bank near the Point of Ayre, off the Isle of Man, where the vessel remained *in statu quo* for one hour before she could be got off the impediment now known as " King William's Bank." The embarkation took place from Hoylake, as in those days Liverpool was not considered a safe harbour owing to the strong tides; moreover it was hard of access, for there were no roads for conveyance—the country around Liverpool was an uncultivated waste.

On the wild sea shore, a few miles from Birkenhead, stands Leasowe Castle, once known as " Mockbeggar Castle." It is supposed to have been built in the reign of Queen Elizabeth, by the Earls of Derby, for the accommodation of guests during the races which were formerly held there, and which were of considerable reputation, until they were discontinued in 1760, when they were transferred to Newmarket, and called the Wallasey Stakes. It was at these races

* There is, in West Kirby Church of St. Bridget, a slab of red sandstone, on which is a shield bearing a cross, with eagles for supporters, and surmounted by a coronet, under which is an inscription in Latin to the memory of Johannes Van Zoelen, who died on the 3rd of September, 1689. He was an officer in the army of the Duke of Schomberg, which was encamped at Leasowe in that year. Many coins of William the Third's reign have been found on the camp ground, doubtless left by the soldiers.

at Leasowe in 1683, that the unfortunate Duke of
Monmouth, son of Charles II. by Lucy Waters, rode
his own horse, and won the plate, which he presented
to his godchild, the daughter of the Mayor of Chester,
to whom he had stood sponsor on the previous day.
There is a curious old picture at the Castle represent-
ing a horse race. The winning post is drawn between
the contending horses. The jockeys are in singular
costume, but in coloured jackets and caps. King
James I. and his son, afterwards Charles I. look on. The
courtiers are in full dress, the gentlemen wearing long
dress swords, while the King has only the hilt of one
(This is a curious testimony of the rumour that the
scenes of bloodshed which preceded his birth left
their traces in his nervous system, causing him during
life to regard blood or a sword with horror.) The
capacious royal carriage contains the Queen (Anne of
Denmark) who surveys the sport from the window.
The coachman, in scarlet, drives merely a pair of
horses, and the attendant outriders wear short scarlet
cloaks. A man in a tree, without shoes and stockings,
cheers the winner. The site of the race-course has
been submerged in the devouring element that has
attacked the mainland. The Castle is built in octa-
gonal form, with turrets on the alternate faces; the
carved oak fittings of the famous Star Chamber at
Westminster have here found resting place, being
brought from St. Stephen's Chapel, in 1834; and
the staircase is decorated with a pictorial record of
victories of England, naval and military, between
Blenheim and Waterloo. The library is fitted up with
oak from the submarine forest. To resist the en-
croachments of the sea a solid embankment has been
built. Upon this stands the remains of a little house

formerly used for fish-curing. The inside has been embellished in a curious manner with fish-shells in tasteful designs. On a terrace above the embankment is a rudely carved seat, and in its back is inserted the mandate of Canute that the sea should come no further. From this terrace during the sun's solstice it can be seen to both rise and set in the sea. Owing to the inroads made by the tides, Leasowe Lighthouse has twice been removed inland. Leasowe Castle was purchased from the Egertons by the widow of Lewis Boote, Esq., whose only daughter and heiress married the late Sir E. C——, in 1821. In spite of certain eccentricities, Lady C—— was an eminently charitable woman, as many an humble cottager could testify. The Birkenhead Hospital was at one time in Hamilton Street, she was a constant visitor, and gave ample evidence of her kind heart in the bountiful and useful gifts she made to the institution. She was very unpretentious, and mostly came to market in a very ordinary lilac print dress. She would purchase an odd or end of china for household purposes saying, "Never mind the paper," hide it under her large red Galway cloak, and walk away to her splendid carriage, and attendant spotted dogs. Her ladyship had a mania for cats, and would have as many as a hundred or more living together in harmony in a building adjoining the Castle. Their recreation ground was wired round. One special favourite was an Angora, named "Prince Charlie"—he constantly accompanied his mistress in her drives, placing his paws on the window of the carriage while he looked out on the humanity that envied him his luxurious berth. A female attendant was engaged to superintend the comfort of the feline community. Lady C—— was highly accomplished, and the memorial she executed to the memory of her daughter in Bidston Church, testifies to her ability as a wood-carver.

In the early days of the Volunteers, Lady C——offered to present the 2nd Cheshire corps with a bugle. On the march out to Leasowe many ladies accompanied, and, though the atmosphere proved raw and drizzling, the great gates of the Castle were closed, and the detachment and escort of fair ones directed to march through the mud to the presentation ground. Here they shivered for half-an-hour, when her ladyship, who was a thorough horsewoman, made her *entrée* on her prancing white charger. After a florid speech about the prospective probabilities of being called to arms to defend the shores of their forefathers, she disappointed them by handing to the bugler a *brass* instrument. They had serious thoughts of leaving the brass bugle behind, and pretending they had forgotten it. A poetical genius among them parodied the march out, and Prince Albert accepted a copy.

CHAPTER XIII.

Parkgate a station for the Irish Packets—Interesting Records—The Death of Dr. Burney's Daughter—Ryley the Itinerant—Handel at Parkgate—An Account of the First Performance of the " Messiah " at Dublin—Primitive Hoylake—Hilbre Island.

In the days when Birkenhead numbered only one hundred inhabitants, Parkgate, on the border of the Dee, was a station of importance, from whence the Irish packets sailed at least three or four times a week. The receding tides, however, necessitated their discontinuance about the year 1810. This diminutive port owned its own Custom House and staff of officials.

The renowned Billy O'Rourke left a record in verse of *his* passage from Dublin. Says he—

> I paid the Captain six thirteens
>   To carry me over to Parkgate ;
> Before we got half over the waves,
>   It blew at a terrible hard rate.
> * * * * *
> Says the sailor, "To the bottom you go!"
>   Says I, "We don't care a farthing,
> For I've paid my passage to Parkgate, you know,
>   And I'll hould you up to your bargain!"

In the year 1784, the embryo lady of title who became renowned as the wife of Sir William Hamilton, visited Parkgate for the cure of an eruptive affection on her arms and knees. The use of salt water three or four times a day, and applications of tang, or sea-weed, effected a complete restoration to health. During her stay, she, her mother, and little girl, were lodged and boarded by a Mrs. Darnwood, for one-and-a-half guineas, and she made them most comfortable, despite her moderate remuneration.

In the early part of the present century, a well-known Chester drawing-master, Mr. Burt, paid an annual visit to Parkgate during the summer months. His mode of conveyance was one of the old-fashioned hobby-horses then in vogue, propelled by the feet, the wheels being specially made for him of barrel hoops for lightness. He always resided in the same house, right opposite to the Chester Arms. It may easily be detected, as the front of the pathway is paved with small pebbles, the groundwork of yellow throw up the the name NELSON in black.

This was the work of Burt, who gathered the stones on the shore, and spent his leisure moments in inserting this lasting memento of the great admiral, of whom he had executed a couple of engravings. The top part of the first two letters has been cut off, to enable a bow window to replace a straight one. The little house has another interesting relic scratched on the panes of glass in a front window, thus—

Ann Guile N

29

N November 1783

Ann Guile was said to have been crossed in love, dying of a broken heart, her truant lover defraying the expenses of an attendant as she faded away. A policeman, named John Moore, has endeavoured to memorialise himself by scratching his name also, but has given up his task from incompetence, the two letters O in his name having shaped themselves in decided squares, whereon he retired in disgust, leaving the word unfinished. The house is now in the occupation of the county constabulary.

Letters from Ireland were sent to England *via* Parkgate as opportunity served. From thence they were conveyed in chaises to Chester, and there sorted and forwarded to their addresses. The postal packets arrived by these means as often in the night as in the day, and the Chester postmaster and his one clerk were frequently aroused in the small hours of the night to charge the postage on letters so received. Their occupation was lit up only by miserable candle-light, as gas-light was then unknown.

We have record of another interesting visitor who came over from Ireland, but who, sad to say, died at Parkgate. Susannah Elizabeth, third daughter of Dr. Burney, and wife of Major Phillips, Belcotton, Ireland, was on her way to visit her father at Chelsea College, when she was seized with illness at Parkgate, which proved fatal on January 6, 1800. She was interred in Neston churchyard, and Dr. Burney wrote the following epitaph for the headstone :—

> Learn, pensive reader, who may pass this way,
> That underneath this stone remains the clay
> That held a soul as pure, inform'd, refin'd,
> As e'er to erring mortal was assign'd.

> Closed are the eyes whose radiance mild, yet bright,
> Beamed all that gives to feeling souls delight!
> Quench'd are those rays of spirit, taste, and sense,
> Pure emanations of benevolence,
> That could alike instruct, appease, control,
> And speak the genuine dictates of the soul.   C. B.

The visitors were then sufficiently numerous to encourage histrionic ability. The theatre had formerly been a herring house, when herrings were abundant, and Government gave a bounty for curing them. In the bathing season, an itinerant actor, named Ryley, gave a series of entertainments. His favourite piece he called "His Brooms," in which a number of pasteboard figures made ridiculous grimaces, worked by mechanical process, while he played the violin, and sang a ditty of his own composition, the chorus to which was, "Make faces, make faces." He lived in the deserted house of the look-out Custom House officer, whose services were no longer required, and the romantic little tenement became known as Ryley's Castle. The genial old actor must be regarded as an anomaly, for he actually lived in harmony with, and respected, his mother-in-law, of whom he thus wrote:—"The filial affection of Anne (his wife) had augmented our family by the addition of her mother, and the hurry and bustle of itineracy being ill-adapted for one whose age required quiet and repose, I took a small cottage at Parkgate, in Cheshire, at the annual rent of five pounds. Here I placed my mother-in-law, and here, thank God! she is at this moment." Dear old Ryley, you were missed when you went!

The now unassuming seaside village of Parkgate was one hundred and fifty years ago the resort of families of fashion, or, as they were termed in those days, "the quality," and many persons broke their journey *en route* for Ireland to enjoy the clear, pure air, and quietude of that hamlet by the sea, with its broad flowing Dee, and margin of lovely Welsh scenery. Many of note were among the loiterers; but such associations are rapidly fading from the local mind, little heed give

they to the fact that in one of those humble tenements, for they *are* mostly humble, or was it at the
Mostyn Hotel, now a boarding school, that Handel
rested on his way to Dublin, detained by contrary
winds, and composed a portion of his sacred triumph
that shall be sung by men for all ages, the sublime
oratorio of "The Messiah." The house itself has been
lost sight of, but it is a certainty that Handel wrote
some of his score as he halted there for a few brief
days, going from Parkgate to Chester, to try the effect
of his song of faith, " I know that my Redeemer
liveth" on its magnificent Cathedral organ. Dr.
Burney, as a boy of fifteen, saw Handel in Chester on
this memorable journey, and, with his own precocious
musical enthusiasm, he tells us how "I watched him
narrowly as long as he remained in Chester, which, on
account of the wind being unfavourable at Parkgate,
was several days." The great composer applied to
Mr. Baker, the organist, to know whether any of the
choirmen could sing at sight, as he wished to prove
some books that had been hastily transcribed, by
trying the choruses which he intended to perform in
Ireland, Mr. Baker mentioned the likeliest men in
Chester, and these met for rehearsal at the " Golden
Falcon," where Handel had put up. On trial, the
impromptu chorus signally failed in their rendering
of "And with his stripes we are healed," which,
Dr. Burney says, " caused Handel to swear in five
languages."

The first performance of this great work was given
at the New Music Hall, Fishamble Street, Dublin, on
April 13th, 1742, in the sacred cause of charity for the
benefit of the poor, the sick, and miserable prisoners
for debt. The announcement was received with so

much favour that an advertisement was issued beg-
ging ladies to attend unencumbered by their hoops,
and gentlemen minus their swords, which concession
enabled the stewards to seat 700 people instead of
600, with the gratifying result that £400 was divided
among the three aforenamed charities.

When the oratorio was performed for the first
time in London, at Covent Garden, on March 23rd,
1743, the audience were so moved with enthusiasm
as they heard the elevating strains of the glorious
Hallelujah Chorus that they involuntarily rose with
one accord, headed by His Majesty George the
Second, and stood until its conclusion, which reverent
custom is observed to this day.

We have the authority of Dr. Allott, Dean of
Raphoe, that when Handel was questioned as to
what influence he was under when he composed the
" Messiah," he replied, " I did think I did see all
Heaven before me, and the great GOD himself."

Little did the simple fisherfolk of Parkgate recog-
nise the genius that walked in their midst ; they only
called him " the foreign gentleman," from the guttural
language he used as he strolled among them on the
beach.

As Hoylake is now the summer residence of most
of the Birkenhead families, it will not be considered
further digression to include it in this chapter.

About the year 1860, Hoylake began its career as a
rendezvous for seaside residents. The only mode of
conveyance was the old omnibus " Atlas," which
started from the yard of Gough's Woodside Hotel,
morning and afternoon, its arrival in the little village
serving as the chief item of interest in daily life. I
remember my first journey in it, accompanying my

mother to seek a temporary house. Heavy rains had flooded the roads to such an extent that they looked like a canal. As a rule, the omnibus discharged its passengers on the corner now occupied by the Stanley Hotel, and then proceeded to lay up at the Green Lodge Hotel, the ground between these two points being too uneven for pleasant locomotion. But on this special day, the pent-up passengers resembled the inmates of the ark, for there was no ground whereon to set foot, and, *nolens volens*, we were driven (holding on) into the yard of the Green Lodge, and deposited in the kitchen. The landlady, informed of our arrival, called out, " Show them to Mr. Samuel's room." The chief works of art in this accommodating apartment were replicas of mine hostess as a bride. She seemed to keep an eye upon us from all points. Presently we heard the landlord told to go an errand. " I can't," said he, " it's raining." " Put on Mr. Samuel's coat," said the landlady, whereon we saw him obediently stem the flood in the borrowed garment. There was no library in those days, and nothing to eat unless it was bespoken. " I'll take that," said my mother to the only butcher, pointing to the only joint on the block. " No you won't," said the burly purveyor, " it's ordered." On the day after our arrival we were literally hard up for a dinner.

Oh, what a dreary place it was ! No one to speak to, the fisherpeople clannish; and so depressed did we become that one day my sister and I actually sat on an upturned boat and cried for want of something to do. We would have been thankful if some of the women had given us some sewing.

On the occasion of our first visit, the fields were covered with excrescences closely resembling mush-

rooms, of which there is now no trace. I had a
narrow escape of giving my relatives what the an-
cients would have termed " a potion," for I had
collected a fair cargo of the poisons whereon to
regale them. The happy intervention of a plough-
man fortunately prevented the extermination of our
race.

In 1784, Amy Lyon, who was destined to become
Lady Hamilton, and who, by the way, was a native of
Neston, wrote of Hoylake, from Parkgate, where she
was staying, that High Lake (as it was then called)
only contained three houses, not fit for a Christian to
live in, and a public house, which was the resort
of such sailors as had to put in through stress of
weather. This would most probably be the " Ship
Inn," still standing in Market Street, and as great
a favourite with present day toilers of the sea as ever
it was with their predecessors. Fifty years ago, the
place had made little progress towards habitation.

One sad and dreary day, in the year 1848, the
inflowing tide bore a ghastly burden, and deposited it
on the beach of that primitive village. Fifty bodies
of those who were on the ill-fated vessel, *Ocean
Monarch*, when she was burnt off the Orme's Head,
were washed ashore at Hoylake.

The church at Hoylake was erected from the
designs of Mr. (afterwards Sir) James Picton, who
copied the windows of the nave and west front from
an old Norman Church at Castle Rising, in Norfolk.
Some curious epitaphs have emanated from the hand
of the local stonemason on the tombstones in the
churchyard.

In 1860 the annual races were still run. The
grand stand on the now disused race-course was

built by members of the Liverpool Hunt, a club that has ceased to éxist.

Hilbre Island was formerly of holy repute. The Benedictines of St. Werburg established a small cell, dedicated to the Virgin Mary. The visitors to the shrine contributed to their support. There are two caves on the large island; one, "The Lady's Cave;" the other, "The Devil's Hole." There is a legend of a miracle performed in this vicinity for Richard, young Earl of Chester, who was attacked by Welsh marauders as he and his escort were returning from a pilgrimage to St. Winifred's Well. The Earl took sanctuary at the Monastery of Basingwerke until troops arrived to protect him. Upon reaching the shore the Earl prayed to St. Werburg, who was graciously pleased to lend an attentive ear. The waters divided, disclosing a sandbank, over which passed the relieving soldiers, commanded by Fitz-Nigel, Baron of Halton, and Constable of Chester. This incident gave the name to the bank "The Constable's Sands."

The reputation of the island went from one extreme to the other. The altar was replaced by the public-house, the ground was no longer holy, for smugglers, and cock-fighters, drew together many a disreputable concourse.

There is nothing whatever now to invite a visit—the herbage is dried up. My own enterprise was rewarded only with the sight of an eel, a few small crabs, and the destruction of a pair of boots!

CHAPTER XIV.

OLD FRANCIS, OF BEBINGTON—THERE WERE MONSTERS IN THOSE DAYS.

THE house in which the late Joseph Mayer, Esq., F.A.S., first opened his library at Bebington, was formally occupied by a most eccentric individual, one Thomas Francis. In a room he kept the coffins intended for the ultimate use of himself and wife, and when their bodily growth exceeded the original limits of their last home, he had them enlarged to a more comfortable fit. He invariably spent his birthday reclining in his coffin, and his wife must have watched the dawn arise on her natal day with anything but a feeling of welcome, as her eccentric spouse compelled her to moralise within the compass of her final bed in like manner. Evidence of his harmless originalities were to be found at all corners. In his garden he built a tower, and surmounted it with two big wooden guns; his archway in the grounds was decorated with the glass "kecks" of bottles; while, to terrify the trespasser, the stone dog kept guard in his kennel, and still holds the rising generation in check. Over his front door he raised a massive figure of Britannia, with shield and spear, beneath which, in the veran-dah, against the wall, he carved his own effigy, in low crowned hat, knee breeches, and shoes, striking with a hammer a rock topped by a castle; from the fissure he

had cleft there issues a stream of water, and below is
this inscription :—" When the people of Bebington
murmured for water, I cut the rock, and God gave
them plenty," an allusion to his present of a well to
the people of the locality. Under his verandah he
would sit and watch for passers by, whom he would
invite to dine with him, they unwarily accepting his
proffered hospitality only to be disappointed in the
meagre fare of roast sparrow, cockles, and such like
light refreshment, while he calmly enjoyed their
astonishment. To this day, there still remain, in the
boundary wall of his premises, several curious inscrip-
tions cut in stone. This corner was a loitering place
for the village laggards, who leant against it as they
gossiped, and for their admonition he inserted—

<pre>
        " A R
            U B B
        I
            N G S
        T O N E F
            O R A S
        S E
        S "
</pre>

which, being interpreted, readeth thus : " A rubbing
stone for asses."

Another—" Subtract 45 from 45 that 45 may
remain "—is done thus :

987654321—added lengthways, comes to 45.
123456789—added lengthways, comes to 45.

864197532—added lengthways, comes to 45.

A third—

> " From six take nine,
>   From nine take ten,
> From forty take fifty,
>   Then six will remain,"

has this elucidation—

S I X	S ┼─✳	S
I X	I ✳	I
X L	X ㇱ	X

> '' My name And sign
>   is thirty Shillings just,
> And he that will tell
> My Name Shall
>   have a Quart on trust.
> For Why is not Five the Fourth
> Part of Twenty the Same in
> All Cases ? "

bears this solution—

			s.	d.
Name,	Mark	i.e.	13	4
	Noble	,,	6	8
Sign	Two crowns	,,	10	0
			30	0

Mark Noble, of the sign of " The Two Crowns."

Anon—

> " IN [S] MemOR. yof Kathe
> Ry Neg Ray cH ang'd
> FRO. mab. USyli Feto
> li Fele SSClay fromea
> RThan Dcl. Ay.s He go

H

Therp ElfaNd. No WS
He ! stur N'Dtoe. ARt
HHErselF y—E Weep
in Gfr I Ends now
be ADvise Dabate
yoUr Grief & dry your. Eyes."

is an epitaph that bears this translation—

" In sacred memory of Katherine Gray
Changed from a busy life to lifeless clay,
From earth and clay she got her pelf,
And now she's turned to earth herself.
Ye weeping friends, now be advised,
Abate your grief and dry your eyes."

At Storeton, in the vicinity of Birkenhead, there
are extensive freestone quarries, rich in fossils and
traces of antediluvian animals such as the cheirotherium. Impressions which were probably caused by
the crawling or walking of tortoises, lizards, croco-
diles, and the rhynchosaurus, a creature with the
body of a reptile and the beak and feet of a bird, have
constantly been brought to light by the workmen who
labour at the stone. When Storeton rock was in a
semi-liquid state, the monster cheirotherium must
have passed, of which existence is traced to no other
known part but Dumfries. In the quarry, at a depth
of forty feet, a continuous line of its footprints has
been discovered. It had a greater resemblance to a
giant frog than aught else. The feetmarks in the
stone are like enormous human hands, but the fingers
and thumb shorter and thicker, tapering off claw-like.
As the freestone is split up, the layers separate, and
disclose the traces of the monster's progress. The

evidence of the creature's existence in these quarries points to a more recent date than elsewhere; in fact, it was docketed as a fossil in its other quarter before its appearance in this latitude. Writers have thought the great Wirral forest might have been the scene of many of the tales of knight and monster. Who knows?

CHAPTER XV.

THE OLD ABBEY RUINS—TIME, OLD TIME, SHALL BE KING AFTER ALL.

WE have some pretensions to antiquity in the remains of the Benedictine Monastery, dedicated to St. Mary and St. James, which still stand near to Monk's Ferry. Its foundation dates back seven hundred years, the records bearing date 1153. How different was the aspect of the adjacent country in the days when the religious community tilled the land. The greater part of the Hundred of Wirral was one of the Earl of Chester's forests. Woods, rich in dell and dingle, girded the Priory, with its Grange and cultivated strip of land. The little stream of the Birken, or Birket, swelled into a broad pool at its confluence with the Mersey, and gave its name to the new town of Birkenhead. Some years ago, when navvies were excavating in the line of roadway between Birkenhead and Bidston, a most interesting archæological discovery was accidentally made by one of the engineers. Several feet below the surface of the road, a portion of an old wooden bridge, about a hundred feet long, was unearthed, in a wonderful state of preservation. This bridge evidently crossed one of the tributaries of the Birket river, and was, in all probability, the handiwork of the monks at the Priory. In due course, the stream had become dried up, and the bridge buried by the roadway. The oaken beams rested on the rock at

either end, and on intermediate stone piers. Birket
river flowed somewhat in the same direction from
Meols as is now covered by Hoylake Railway, and it

BIRKENHEAD PRIORY.

emptied itself into Wallasey Pool. The Prior of the
Abbey was a personage of considerable importance in
Wirral, ranking with the Barons of the Palatine,

sitting in the Parliament of the Earl of Chester, and seldom riding out without the attendance of his Chamberlain, Marshal and other officers. He claimed rights of fisheries, wreckage, and boats, from the manor of Oxton to the Mersey, with the privilege of ferrying passengers from Birkenhead to Liverpool, a concession derived by letters patent from Edward II. The ferry dues had previously been the perquisite of Edmund, Earl of Lancaster, whose father, Henry III, had given them to him. The Abbot likewise kept an inn for the accommodation of travellers. From ancient archives—a sort of Court Chronicle of royal progress—we learn that Edward I visited the Priory, and slept there two nights, after which he proceeded up the river in the Abbot's barge. This would most probably be about the time when the first Prince of Wales was born at Carnarvon, and Edward made a tour in the provinces to conciliate the people whom he had subjugated.

The Island of Hilbre had its shrine of "Our Ladye of Hilbree," which attracted many devotees from the neighbouring "hamlet of Lyverpol," * who made use of the Monk's Ferry (a name it still bears) in going to and returning from their religious pilgrimages. A beacon lighted on the opposite shore was the signal to the monks to send over a boat for passengers.

At the dissolution of monasteries in 1536, Birkenhead was one of the first that fell. The property of Prior and Monks, riches, dues, convent, belfry, grange,

* Lyverpol, or Lytherpol, was the name of the seaport at the same period that Hoylake was known as Hegh Pol, which will be read as High Pool and Lower Pool. The *locale* of Hoylake was much more important at that date than Liverpool. Owing to the slight depth of water at the entrance of the Mersey, ships had to discharge part of their cargo at Wallasey, and, thus lightened, were enabled to proceed up the river to the port.

ferry house, &c., passed, first into the hands of Henry VIII, and afterwards to one Ralph Worsley. The dislodged monks were provided with forty shillings each and a new gown; some earned a livelihood by bookbinding, others by singing at Waller on the Sea * or Bidstone, and the remainder by more menial employments as best they could. The revenue at the time of the monks' expulsion was £100, equal now to £2,000.

Tradition states that they made an effort to conceal their treasure at this period, and stored their plate in a subterranean passage leading to the river. The story tells that a large well-balanced stone occupied the centre of the passage as a door, but during the flight of the monks it gave way, killing one and cutting off the retreat of another, whose bones are supposed to lie hidden with the treasure in the tunnel. No indication of the secret subway or its valuable contents has ever been discovered.

In the year 1818, a great stone was dug up, that had evidently marked the last resting place of the vicar, Thomas Rayneford, who was inducted to the Priory in 1460; beneath it lay three skeletons in a very perfect condition. The inscription, in Church-text, which runs round the edge as a border, thus translates: " Here lieth Thomas Rayneford, formerly the good vicar of this house, who died 20th May, in the year of our Lord, 1473. On whose soul may God have mercy." This stone has been inserted into the wall of the chapter-house, in an upright position, by the entrance door. This edifice, which is the oldest of the buildings, is in the best preservation, being intact. With the departure of the monks, this corner of the

* Wallasey.

Peninsula of Wirral sank into insignificance, and so remained for two hundred and fifty years, when it arose so unexpectedly and rapidly as to be termed a town of mushroom growth.

All that remains of the ancient Priory is a small portion of the west wall of the church, with traces of the stairs leading to the Prior's apartments: the refectory and room apportioned to the Prior, the crypt and kitchen below, and the dormitory above, together with the aforesaid chapter-house. The ruins are exceedingly pretty—roofless, save the chapter-house, the decaying walls topped by a profusion of graceful creeping plants which trail in wild elegance among the mouldering stones. Upon these sacred relics old King Time has surely set his mark. The hands which hospitably tended the weary and footsore wayfarer in the days of toilsome travel, have been stilled for many a year; the oars with which the lay brothers rippled the surface of Mersey river have long been cast aside for ever. All—all has been subjected to the inevitable law of change.

At the commencement of the present century, the old Priory ruins stood in picturesque isolation, a prominent feature in the landscape, and they now repose in our midst an incontestable evidence of the progress of science and civilisation. At so recent a period as seventy-five years ago, the hamlet of Birkenhead numbered only a hundred inhabitants, who abode in three houses, and a few scattered cottages, which were the sole erections in this now extensive port. So magnified has it become that cabs, gas bills, and water rates are as common in the district as were formerly oaks and squirrels. All rural felicity has vanished with the advent of the knight of bricks and mortar.

Where once the sweet harmony of matins and vespers alone broke the silence that reigned around, the din and clang of weighty hammers resound, and the roar of machinery smites the ear with deafening noise, as a thousand workmen shape the ocean-going steamers bound for lands unknown and undreamt of by the humble monks. Shipyards and manufactories have replaced the tillers of the soil; massive steamers plough through the waters, transferring thousands of passengers from shore to shore, have succeeded the primitive ferry-boat of the Benedictines. Industry has encroached upon the old Monastery, and so environed it as if it would compress and crush it out. A passing stranger would pause, and gaze with astonishment to find a ruin so completely encompassed by modern tenements.

Old King Time is asserting his right, and stealing it gradually from us. Decay is craftily undermining our solitary pretensions to antiquity, beautifying its act of destruction by natural growth that marks its ancient claims. Surely some effort will be made to retain the one link between the busy work-a-day world and the far past when the few dwellers tilled the ground, and lived together in brotherly love. The magnificence of no modern structure impresses the mind with the same elevated sentiment as does the deserted ruin of monastic type, grand and sublime in its decline, with its flower-crowned walls bereft of roofing, canopied alone by heaven. We picture the solemnity of religious services, the aiming at goodness, and practical Christian charity exercised within its bounds, and a better feeling arises, no matter what our creed, to respect the holy dead, and preserve their handiwork for our own honour's sake, and atone, as far as possible, for the barbarous act of demolition. Let us show, with pardonable pride, our claim to honourable mention in the old records of our country, for antiquity is the essence of respectability, and the possession of such a trophy will materially increase our distinction if the time should ever arrive when we have consummated the prophecy—cast aside the prospective, and become the people of " the City."

May that day be not long distant, and may the dwellers herein be sojourners in the land when the great forecast is realised.

THE END.

PRINTED BY EDWARD HOWELL, CHURCH STREET, LIVERPOOL.

THE
MERSEY COAL COMPANY
Colliery Owners & Merchants,
BIRKENHEAD AND SEACOMBE.

OFFICES—
92 ARGYLE STREET, BIRKENHEAD
AND THE FERRY, SEACOMBE.

BRANCHES—
13 OXTON ROAD, BIRKENHEAD
AND WALLASEY STATION.

WHARVES—
8 ABBEY STREET, BIRKENHEAD
AND BIRKENHEAD ROAD, SEACOMBE.

Special Quotations for Wagon Loads, and Special Discount for Cash before or on Delivery.

Their own "GATEWEN" MAIN COAL is universally liked, and is largely used as a Best KITCHEN COAL.

The **MERSEY COAL COMPANY** pride themselves upon the promptitude of delivery of orders entrusted to them.

SEND FOR PRICE LIST.

Michael Byrne

123 GRANGE ROAD,

Birkenhead.

Family and Shipping Butcher.

HOTELS, PUBLIC INSTITUTIONS, AND FAMILIES
SPECIALLY CONTRACTED FOR.

Corned Beef and Pickled Tongues
ALWAYS ON HAND.

N.B.—Joints Sent Free any distance.

M. HARKER

Confectioner,

AND

FANCY BREAD

BAKER,

35 GRANGE ROAD WEST,

BIRKENHEAD.

*Tea Parties and Balls catered for
on the shortest notice.*

RICH BRIDES' CAKES
MADE TO ORDER.

TELEPHONE No. 4258.

HIGGINS & SMITH

UNDERTAKERS

AND

FUNERAL CARRIAGE PROPRIETORS,

132 CHESTER ST.

40 WATSON ST.

AND

15 PRIORY ST.

BIRKENHEAD.

FUNERALS FURNISHED & DIRECTED
WITH REFINEMENT AND
ECONOMY

MRS. JAMES

𝔖𝔢𝔯𝔟𝔞𝔫𝔱𝔰' 𝔎𝔢𝔤𝔦𝔰𝔱𝔯𝔶 𝔄𝔭𝔭𝔬𝔦𝔫𝔱𝔪𝔢𝔫𝔱 𝔎𝔬𝔬𝔪𝔰

36 GRANGE ROAD WEST,

BIRKENHEAD.

Superior Servants waiting to be engaged.

J. JONES & CO.

FASHIONABLE TAILORS

HATTERS AND OUTFITTERS

"THE PARAGON,"

158 & 160 GRANGE ROAD

BIRKENHEAD.

Naval and Military Uniforms made on the Shortest Notice.

ESTABLISHED 1864.

LACKLAND & CO.

𝔚indow 𝔊lass 𝔐erchants

FOR HOME USE AND EXPORTATION.

Manufacturers of every description of

STAINED GLASS

Glazing Executed in all parts of the Country.

14, 16 & 18 CONWAY STREET

AND

89 ARGYLE STREET

𝔅irkenhead.

W. C. PASHLEY

56 ARGYLE STREET

BIRKENHEAD.

CARVER AND GILDER,

Picture Frame and Window Cornice

MANUFACTURER,

DEALER IN ARTIST'S MATERIALS

&c., &c.

ROBB BROTHERS,

GENERAL DRAPERS,

Ladies' & Gentlemen's Outfitters,

ARE NOW SHOWING THE

LATEST NOVELTIES

IN

DRESS FABRICS

AND

GENERAL

HOUSEHOLD DRAPERY.

New Goods in all Departments.

CROSS STREET & GRANGE ROAD,

BIRKENHEAD.

A CHEERFUL OLD SOUL.

IS IT POSSIBLE

for a woman with increasing years to do laundry work. Thousands who would have been laid aside under the old system of washing have proved what

SUNLIGHT SOAP

can do in reducing labour. The cleansing properties of SUNLIGHT SOAP save years of arduous toil. Reader, prove SUNLIGHT SOAP for yourself.

BEWARE.—Do not allow other Soaps, said to be the same as the "SUNLIGHT SOAP," to be palmed off upon you. If you do you must expect to be disappointed. See that you get what you ask for, and that the word "SUNLIGHT" is stamped upon every tablet, and printed upon every wrapper.

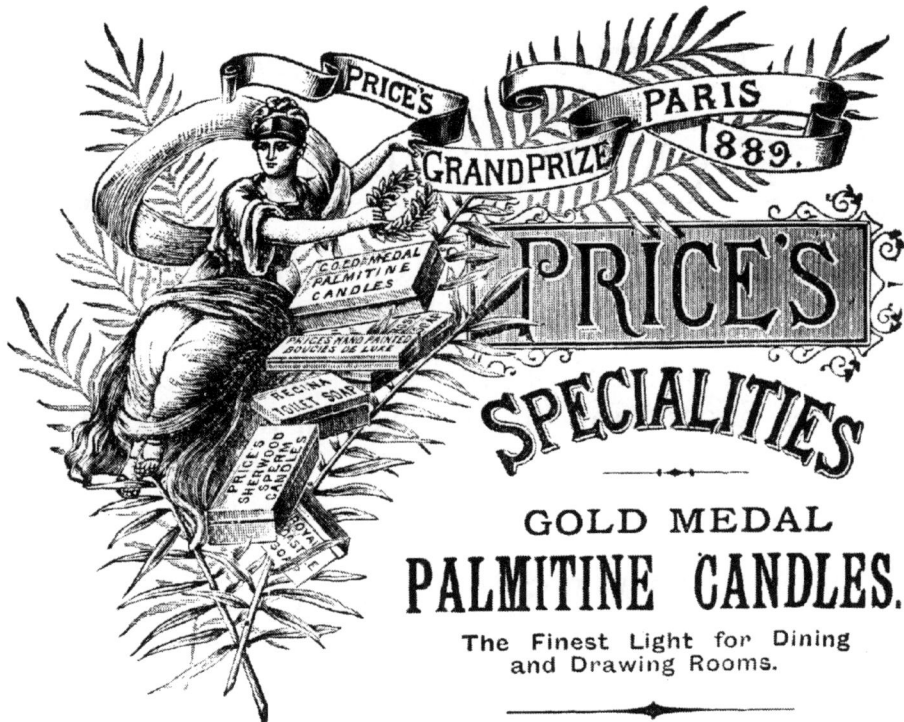

PRICE'S GRAND PRIZE PARIS 1889.

PRICE'S

SPECIALITIES

GOLD MEDAL
PALMITINE CANDLES.

The Finest Light for Dining
and Drawing Rooms.

NIGHT LIGHTS

"CHILDS',"

"NEW PATENT", "ROYAL CASTLE."

"REGINA"
THE QUEEN OF TOILET SOAPS.

PRICE'S GLYCERINE
FOR MEDICINAL USE
GUARANTEED FREE FROM ARSENIC
AND ALL OTHER IMPURITIES.

PRICE'S PATENT CANDLE COMPANY LIMITED.

Works published by Mr. Howell—continued.

By FRANCES PARTHENOPE (LADY VERNEY).

II.—ESSAYS AND TALES. Thick vol., crown 8vo. with Frontispiece, "Claydon House" cloth gilt, 10s. 6d.

By SAMUEL TAYLOR COLERIDGE

I.—AIDS TO REFLECTION IN THE FORMATION of a Manly Character, or the several grounds of Prudence, Morality and Religion. New Edition, with copious Index, and Translations of the Greek and Latin Quotations by Thomas Fenby. Post 8vo, cloth, 2s. 6d.

II.—SHAKESPEARE, BEN JONSON, BEAUMONT and Fletcher. NOTES AND LECTURES on the OLD DRAMATISTS. New Edition, post 8vo, cloth gilt, 2s. 6d.

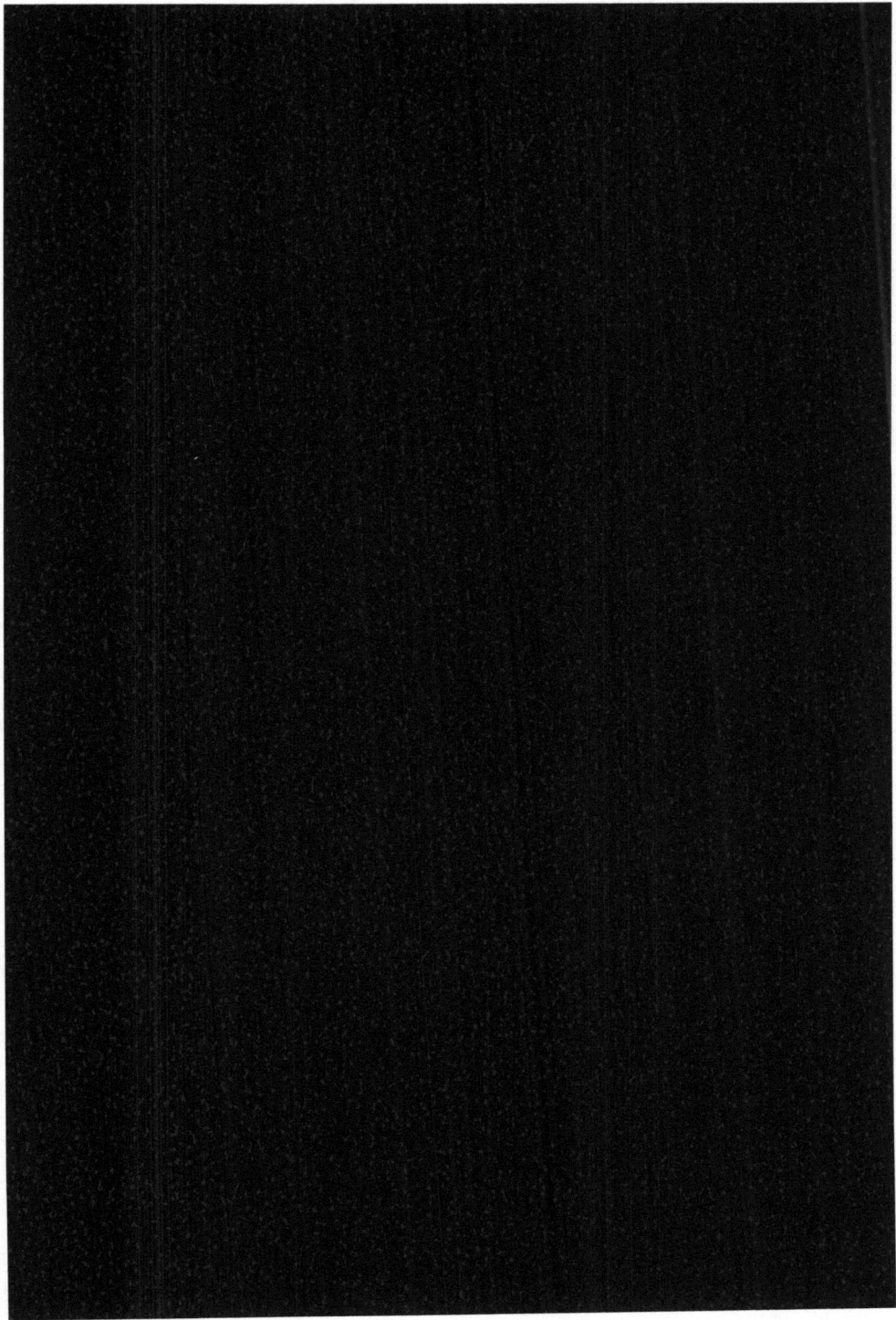

Milton Keynes UK
Ingram Content Group UK Ltd.
UKHW032202131223
434291UK00009B/619